Confessions of a Preacher's Wife

Confessions of a Preacher's Wife

by
Pauline E. Spray

Beacon Hill Press of Kansas City
Kansas City, Missouri

ISBN: 083-410-9395

Printed in the United States of America

Cover art: Royce Ratcliff

10 9 8 7 6 5 4 3 2 1

Dedication

To the memory of
J. Wesley and Maudie Spray,
without whose contribution to posterity
this story could not have been written.

Contents

From my scrapbook . . .

The Minister's Wife

Her churchly presence was exemplary
And to the congregation gave no sign
That when he read, "Blessed are the meek . . ."
Her thoughts dwelt on the contour of his cheek—
That when he preached of punishment and hell,
She mused on how his head was shaped so well.
—POLLY PRICE MADDEN

But First, Let Me Explain . . .

You might say preachers run in the family. Dad began preaching when he was 18 and at 85 continued to fill a pulpit occasionally and conduct numerous funerals and weddings. My husband is a clergyman, too, as are two brothers, a son-in-law, two nephews, with more in various stages of ecclesiastical development.

Writers are told to stick to what they know, to write about subjects with which they are familiar. Therefore, it is only natural that I should choose to vociferate about life in the parsonage, having spent the greater part of my earthly existence in one—or another.

In the following pages I have endeavored to exalt God by giving an account of some of the miracles He has wrought in the lives of my husband and myself. In fact, finding each other was a miracle.

Seeking to relate our story as truthfully as possible was not accomplished without a sense of trepidation, however. Life is not all good. Nor is it all bad. It is a mixture of both. To be realistic a story must be told like it is, including both the agreeable and the disagreeable. Exposing some experiences may hurt a few. Nevertheless, the baring of them may also serve to help and encourage others. The latter is my hope and prayer, for I have endeavored to write in the spirit of love. Certainly this confession is not intended to be a venomous catharsis.

After much of the manuscript was completed, I seriously questioned whether to submit it for publication.

"Lord, will it hurt more than it will help?" I asked.

My answer came almost immediately when I was directed to some words by Emmelyn Helsel. Commenting on the 114th psalm, she said: "The Psalmist . . . wanted his people never to forget from whence they had come. They must remember how wonderfully God had blessed them. . . .

"With them we review God's workings in our past. From that heritage we gain fresh courage and greater faith to believe that whatever the future holds God will see us through."

Life is not growing easier for the Christian—clergy or laity. As the second coming of Jesus Christ approaches, Satan is working harder than ever to defeat God's plans and afflict His children. Therefore, if the recounting of the miracles in our lives serves to strengthen not only our own faith and that of our posterity, but the faith of others as well, we shall have achieved our goal.

To protect any who may be injured or embarrassed, fictitious names have been used liberally.

In relating the unpleasant experiences which gave rise to God's miracles of deliverance and victory, it may seem we concentrated more on the negative than the positive aspects of our ministry. As is usually the case, the naughty boy draws more attention than an obedient, docile son.

For over 32 years my husband and I enjoyed wonderful fellowship with a host of God's chosen laity. Scores of dedicated Christians contributed liberally of their time, energy, and resources to please us. These friendships have given (and continue to give us) much pleasure and are greatly appreciated.

Furthermore, serving the Lord and doing His will (wherever it finds one) brings true fulfillment. His indwelling presence turns our nights of tribulation into mornings of praise, the most demanding journey into a joyful one.

To all who helped in any way to produce this confession, I am indebted. I wish to thank my parents for giving me love, a fun-filled childhood, and introducing me to Jesus. Also, much credit is due our daughters, Sybil and Sue, who have afforded us great comfort and delight. Then, to my husband of over 45 years, Russell E. Spray, with whom I lived this story, my continued loyalty and devotion.

"And thou shalt remember all the way which the Lord thy God led thee these forty [plus] years" (Deut. 8:2).

"One generation shall praise thy works to another, and shall declare thy mighty acts" (Ps. 145:4).

1

First Miracle

"Did you see the revival bill?" Ma asked shortly after I came in from high school on a frigid wintry day.

"Where?"

"Pinned to the curtain in the front room," she answered, poking another stick of firewood into the greedy kitchen range.

The sand-colored announcement, bearing the photographs of two men, publicized the forthcoming revival meeting to be held at Beulah, the country church a few miles east, where my father had preached before taking a temporary leave from the pastorate.

Services were scheduled to begin the fourth of March, according to the advertisement, and continue two weeks. (This eventually was extended to three by common consent of pastor and people.)

The workers went by their last names, "Jay and Spray," a catchy appellation for a unique preaching, instrument-playing, singing duo.

"What do you think? The singer is a pretty good-looking fellow, isn't he?" my soft, round mother asked.

"Oh, he's probably married and got a couple of kids," I replied flippantly. But I didn't tell Ma I had taken more than a nominal interest in his picture.

However, disregarding that momentary pull of gravitation, I was not overcome by excitement about meeting the young singer. Besides, my baby brother was sick with the whooping cough, so I urged Ma to attend the first service of the meeting. I stayed with Jimmy, oblivious to the emotive alteration I would undergo shortly.

When my family returned home that evening, they voiced generous approval of the evangelists. Over bowls of homemade bread and milk, sprinkled liberally with sugar, they talked enthusiastically about the workers. Their glowing reports quickly nixed my nonchalance.

The older member of the team, a lumbering, raw-boned, graying man, preached from a large prophetic chart which hung on the wall behind the pulpit, they said. Brother Jay also played the guitar while singing with his coworker.

According to my family, Buddy Spray was a spirited song director and a whiz of a mandolin player. Furthermore, he was young, handsome—and single.

Yes, single!

Need I add, the second night proved a far different story. It took no coaxing from Ma for me to attend the meeting. Ashamed as I am now to confess it, she missed out on the entire remainder of that crusade. Contrariwise, I skipped nary another night.

And for good reason! When I entered the simply furnished church auditorium that fifth day of March evening, something incredible happened. The wooden pews, bare floor, coal-burning heater, high ceiling, unadorned windows, and the rail-enclosed platform with its upright piano remained the same. Yet, as if touched by a fairy's wand, my world was magically transformed.

The instant I spied the black-headed, immaculate youth on the platform, an inner bell tolled. An unmistakable conviction gripped me. My blue eyes were looking into the brown eyes of the man I was destined to marry. He was the one, and there was no doubt about it. If there is such a thing, then it was love at first sight—for me.

16

Much later I learned, however, that the young evangelist had heard no bells tolling as I did that evening. And not much wonder. I was so bashful I blushed crimson. Layers of crimson, no less. My depression days' coat was a hand-me-down tweed, and my shoes were completely worn through on the bottom. Each morning I cut new innersoles from cardboard to keep my feet off the frozen ground, and after the celluloid peeled off, I ritualistically covered the wooden heels with shoe polish.

But still, the young man, who received the adulation of attractive maidens wherever he went, must have found something interesting about this shy, country lass. Each evening following the invitation, he intercepted me as I left the piano.

"Pauline, it doesn't look good for you to stand on the platform and talk to the singer like you do," my father reprimanded me one evening following the service.

"But Daddy," I insisted, blushing as usual, "I can't help it. He asks me to talk to him."

Before the meeting was over, Buddy Spray and I had sung our first duet, "Every Bridge Is Burned Behind Me," quite oblivious to the prophetic implication involved.

I sat across the table from Buddy when the evangelists dined with us—probably too excited to eat for once in my life. But I still remember what Ma served that day. Tuna was considered quite a delicacy to us then, and she used it in a new recipe. Although the result was disappointing and humiliating to my mother, our guests expressed only hearty approval.

The Sunday our pastor's wife invited me to take dinner with them and spend the afternoon at the parsonage with the workers was a glorious day for me. Certainly her husband had no inkling of what he was instigating when he perused the list of available evangelists and called "Jay and Spray" without first consulting his church board. It brought him criticism, but now I can see it was all a part of God's plan for our lives.

Up to that point, I confess, it looked like I was doomed to spinsterhood. I did not then, nor do I now, believe it is a good idea for Christian young people to date non-Christians. And Christian boys were as scarce, if not scarcer, than hens' teeth in our community. Nevertheless, I need not have been concerned. God was watching out for me. He who notes the sparrow's fall, who knows the exact number of hairs in each head, would provide—if He had to bring me a traveling song evangelist from Oklahoma, 1,200 miles away.

Oklahoma—until I met Buddy the only firsthand knowledge I had ever received about that distant state was from my geography book and a couple of schoolmates who came from there to live with their grandparents and attend our school. (I never forgot them because they brought along some curious-looking toads. Who can say which had impressed me most—the towheaded 12-year-old or the ugly, insectivorous lizards with hornlike spines running along their backs?)

When the revival meeting finally came to a close and it was time for the workers to leave, I was catapulted into supernal bliss when Buddy suggested we continue our friendship via the postal route. After exchanging a few letters, however, the missiles stopped coming, and it seemed that our romance, like a glowing meteorite, had flashed briefly and brilliantly and then disintegrated into nothingness.

Still, there were those who would not let me forget.

Later that spring I finished high school. For a graduation gift my longtime Sunday School teacher gave me a lovely cut glass compote. "This dish will hold just enough Jell-O for you and Buddy Spray," Mrs. Watkins suggested.

Neither would little Jimmy let me wipe the memory of the youthful song evangelist from my mind. For months following the March revival, our enjoyable toddler strummed on a fly sprayer which he carried around the house cradled in his arm. "I'm Buddy 'pray," he declared over and over again, rapping on his imaginary mandolin.

That fall I enrolled in County Normal to learn how to become a schoolmarm. Although Dad had set his heart on having a teacher in the family, I told Ma emphatically, "I'll teach two years and then I'm quitting." Most of our lady acquaintances who were schoolteachers were also "unclaimed blessings," and I was determined not to join their ranks if I could help it. Again, I should not have been anxious.

One afternoon during the summer before beginning to teach in September, while working (and praying) in the garden, I felt impressed to write to Buddy. I freely confess it was considered brash for a girl to take the initiative in those days, but I could not resist the insistent urge.

Upstairs in my room at the end of the hall, the one I shared with my only sister, I dashed off a friendly letter and, disregarding social taboo, mailed it to the young evangelist at his home address. My aberrant action brought a response and a resumption of our correspondence.

Unbeknownst to me, Buddy had not forgotten either. His traveling companion had forced him to think of me rather often, in fact. "That Mellish girl up north is the one for you," Brother Jay insisted.

Naturally, Buddy met many pretty girls in his travels, and some of these acquaintances evoked infatuations. But he was always brought back down to earth by the older man's injunction: "Buddy! Buddy! How many times have I told you—that Mellish girl . . . is the one for you!"

After we resumed our correspondence, Buddy's communications were frequent and nonstop. His letters bore many strange postmarks as he and Brother Jay continued their travels in distant states.

In late autumn or early winter Buddy suggested spending Christmas with our family, and I was overjoyed. I was earning $80.00 a month. Much of this went for other obligations, but out of my limited spending money, I made a significant purchase—a tie clasp bearing the initials R. E. S.

Then a greater amount purchased my first complete store-bought outfit—an ombré-toned burgundy coat, a matching dress with pleated skirt and embroidered bodice, shoes, and purse, also in the same shade. But when I went to meet my sweetheart at the train, I was wearing a gray herringbone skirt—one I had fashioned from a pair of castoff trousers. And having developed a run in my own stockings, I had confiscated my sister's, the first pair of nylons she ever owned. I surmise that even to this day she resents the fact that I put a run in her precious hosiery. Nor can I blame her.

When the week was over, Buddy was glad he had heeded Brother Jay's advice. As the rumbling locomotive headed out of town on its way back to Oklahoma, I dissolved into tears. And aboard the train, Buddy also sought out a secluded spot to give vent to his emotions. By then we both recognized that either one of our lives would be incomplete without the other.

Therefore, on March 8, 1940, two years after I fell in love at first sight (and before my very first year of teaching was completed), we were married in the same country church, surrounded by snowbanks and lulled by a moaning March wind, where we met.

Despite Buddy's aversion to cold weather, he braved the snowbanks and frigid wind to make me his bride. And I, wearing a homemade satin gown and Aunt Lillie's bridal veil, and carrying a bouquet of Easter lilies, took him to be my wedded husband till death us do part.

Thus, God worked His first miracle in our life together. And it was only the beginning.

2

God's Appointment

Despite his experience in the field of song evangelism, my husband was 30 years old before the Lord called him to preach the gospel. For Buddy it was not merely a matter of choosing a life's profession but a fact of divine appointment.

*   *   *

Three weeks after our wedding, Buddy returned to his evangelistic commitments. Since my teaching stint did not end until the latter part of May, I remained behind. But the day following the closing of school, I began my pilgrimage to the small town in southeastern Oklahoma where Jay and Spray were conducting a home mission campaign.

My parents, brothers, and sister accompanied me to the Grand Trunk depot, the same one from which Buddy had departed the latter part of March. There, Ma and Dad watched bravely as I boarded the passenger train. (Although it was the first, it would not be the last time my folks would bid farewell to one of their children at that station. A war was close at hand.)

I confess I have often wondered how Ma and Dad could do it. Of course it was their trust in God that enabled them to let their firstborn go so far away to live with people they (and I) had never seen and knew little about. (Mutual acquaintances, however, had assured us that the Sprays were spiritual and acceptable people, which proved to be definitely true.)

For the long journey I chose to wear the silver-buttoned, black twill suit I had purchased on sale for $5.00; a shiny black sailor, complete with veiling; white gloves; and purse. The latter were prized graduation gifts. To accent my traveling attire a cluster of bright tulips was pinned to my lapel, the parting gift of my beloved friend and maid of honor at our wedding.

"Watch your step, Ma'am," the uniformed, gold-chained conductor cautioned, taking my arm and assisting me on to the mounting stool.

"Take good care of my girl, won't you?" Ma pleaded. Later, when the train was puffing its way west, she gave vent to her grief, her weeping sparked by the single tear she saw coursing down Dad's cheek.

That one tear spoke far more than words, for my father didn't cry easily. (In my whole childhood I saw him weep only once or twice that I remember.) In addition to forfeiting his firstling, a cherished dream was vanishing into thin air along with the smoke of the rumbling locomotive.

To Dad schoolteaching epitomized success and security. Those were days of financial difficulty and great stress. Now that I was situated so as to earn my own money, I could have the material comforts he had been eager but unable to give me.

Carrying a beat-up overnight case, which was secured by a worn leather belt, and the box of lunch Ma had lovingly packed for my many hours on the train, I had climbed aboard with ambivalent feelings. I was anxious to be in Buddy's arms again and feel the warmth of his lips on mine, but it was also difficult to leave Dad. And Ma. We were more like sisters than mother and daughter. I was her "right-hand man," sticking by until the work was done, no matter how late at night.

On Saturdays after working very late, she, my sister, and I bathed beside the kitchen range, the closest thing we had to a bathroom. Always the comedienne (my prize act was doing an imitation fan dance with a dish towel), I kept Ma and Opal in stitches until exhaustion and nausea forced me to bed. Who would make Ma laugh now? Who would help her ready the younger children for bed, cook, scrub, wash, and iron? My sister already had a job in town with little time left to help at home.

And my brothers! How I loved them! I had brooded over them like a fledgling mother hen. Bud, 16 months younger than I, was a slim young man, wearing a hat and vest to see me off. We had been close of spirit as well as of age.

Junior and Paul, "the little boys," as we called them, had been my special charges. Each night for years I had washed their faces, necks, and ears (and overseen their feet washing) before they went to bed.

Little Freddie was almost "my" baby since I was nearly 13 when he was born. Now at 7, he still had a cherubic face. And I had cared for Jimmy, the pet of the family, since he was five days old.

After watching and waving until my loved ones were out of sight, I eventually turned my attention to what was ahead. How would I make it across Chicago—from one station to the other? Would my new husband meet my train in Arkansas the next day? With Ma's warnings ringing in my ears, I was half scared to death.

She had diligently and graphically cautioned me about wicked men who doped young women and carried them off into white slavery. (Grandma Twining had a book in her library that told all about it.) Therefore, my guard was up constantly lest I get too close to a stranger and be injected with a stupefying needle.

Upon reaching Chicago, with the help of a redcap, I was quickly ensconced in a taxi and whisked safely across town. When I was finally aboard the train that would carry me to my destination, I began to breathe easier and settled down to enjoy this fascinating adventure, my first train trip, my first venture outside my home state.

Throughout the inky night, the twisting, jerking locomotive snaked its way over the Ozarks. When we creaked slowly through mountainous Van Buren, someone noted that this was the hometown of the famous comedian Bob Burns.

The next day about noon we screeched to a halt in Fort Smith. There in the clammy, grim, high-ceilinged station Buddy was waiting. He had come from eastern Oklahoma, where he was engaged in a home mission campaign, to meet me.

From Fort Smith a rickety bus bumped us over the Ouachita Mountain roads to the little town where we were to live temporarily. A small white cottage had been provided for the evangelistic party. Immediately I became chief cook and bottle washer.

In spite of the kitchen tasks and washing our clothing by hand on the old-fashioned washboard, life was exciting. Not only was there a honeymoon to resume, I was intrigued by the beautiful area in which we were to spend our first three weeks of housekeeping.

Scrub oak, cedar, hickory, osage orange, sycamore, and locust trees covered the low-lying mountains which rose above the quiet village on three sides. Overhead, fluffy clouds floated aimlessly in the blue expanse. The serene locale, the nightly church services, our plans for life ahead—all added up to a grand adventure for a girl who had scarcely been away from home before. Certainly not this far!

For a time we continued to travel with the evangelist. Nevertheless, it did not take long to recognize the truth of the old adage: Two is company but three (or more) is a crowd. But traveling by ourselves and living off our earnings as song evangelists was asking for mighty poor picking. After the Japanese bombed Pearl Harbor, and a brief stint in college, we headed northward.

There, we eventually rented an apartment. While Buddy engaged in war work, I preened over our three rooms with pride and adulation, rapturously covering orange crates with bright cretonne, and refinishing castoff furniture. Always a homebody, I was in seventh heaven caring for our humble domain. Besides that, my dream of becoming the mother of my own brood was to be fulfilled.

But for my husband it was quite another story. He found himself the victim of a vastly different environment. Until now he had been sheltered from the sordid secular world, having gone directly from school into the evangelistic work. Associating daily with cursing, carousing laborers was shocking emotionally, and spiritually debilitating.

Routine assembly line work was also enervating. Greasy machines held little scope for imagination and inspiration after the excitement of constant travel and soul-winning evangelism. When he transferred to office work, the incessant talk of his foulmouthed peers proved as disgusting as the dirt and grime of the machinery.

After trying for several years to find a satisfactory situation, he finally landed a job which he could reasonably tolerate and almost enjoy. Going to work each day was not quite as difficult; but still, he was far from satisfied with his lot in life.

By this time we had acquired a small house on the outskirts of a large industrial city. It wasn't much but it was ours, and we excitedly set about to remodel it and add on some rooms. Our family was growing and we needed more space.

Nearly four years after Sybil was born, God gave us Sue. With two little girls and a home to care for, my cup of happiness should have been filled to the brim and overflowing. Nevertheless, Buddy's discontentment constantly poked holes in my reservoir of felicity. Although we helped with the music in our local church, nothing could replace the satisfaction and joy he had known while working full-time in the service of the Lord.

"I'm going to take the girls and run over to Hoags for a few minutes," I told him early one spring afternoon.

Outside, the world was beginning to stir, slowly awakening from its long winter's nap. Patches of snow still refused to budge from the accustomed spots, but the warmth of the sun softened the frozen earth and beckoned cheerily.

"Sybil likes to play with Jerry. Besides, it does us good to get out of the house for a little while."

When we returned from our visit, Buddy met us in the kitchen. "I've settled it, Doll," he said bluntly, his eyes still misty.

"What are you talking about?" I asked, tugging at the baby's leggings.

"I've settled it," he repeated.

"Well, what have you settled?" I insisted, not knowing what to expect. Had he decided to pull up stakes and go back to the Southwest? What had happened? What had changed?

"My call to preach," he answered. "I settled it for good this afternoon."

I looked at him questioningly.

He opened his arms and I felt them close about me.

"After you left this afternoon," he said, "I went upstairs to pray."

That was not unusual. He often went to the attic bedroom to pray before going to work on the second shift in midafternoon.

"The Lord showed me definitely today that He wants me to preach," he declared. "I prayed clear through about it."

"That's wonderful!" I cried. "Are you really certain this time?"

"Yes," he said with conviction. "My experience today was as real as when I got saved and sanctified."

26

From the time we were married and even before, Buddy had talked about his desire to preach the gospel. To him preaching the gospel of Jesus Christ was the loftiest of all ambitions, the apex of his aspirations.

But was he called? True, he had thought that he was, perhaps, when he was a teenager, but his single attempt to fill the pulpit had brought discouragement. Ever since that disappointing experience, he had been in doubt. And he had remained unsettled. How could he know for sure? Was or was not his strong desire an indication of God's will for his life? Was his yearning a divine call or was it simply a strong human desire?

Buddy firmly believed that a definite spiritual experience was necessary where a call to preach was concerned. That was what he had been waiting for all these years. Without an explicit encounter, an exceptional assurance from the Lord, he dared not attempt so serious an undertaking.

And rightly so! Later years proved that only a definite God-given appointment would hold my husband steady in times of crisis. Without it he would have reneged on his assignments when the going got rough—and those times were aplenty.

"I've been thinking about that talk Brother Blanchard gave all week," Buddy said. "It has been on my mind ever since Sunday evening. I just can't get away from what he said."

So that did it! My inspiration had worked! Surely it was God-given! (But I'll confess that I did not reveal my secret to Buddy then. Nor for years later. Not until I began writing this book, in fact.)

"I don't want to settle for second place. I want God's best for my life," Buddy insisted.

Living in an unfulfilled and unsettled state of mind had made life difficult for my husband. And for me. His agitation affected both of us adversely. Something needed to happen.

What could be done to bring him to a decision once and for all?

At that time I had charge of the missionary services that were held on the first Sunday evening of each month preceding the regular service. As a part of the program for the previous week I had asked our pastor to bring a short talk on God's call to Christian service. Perhaps, I thought, some word of his might help Buddy resolve the inner conflict with which he had struggled so long.

In giving his remarks our pastor expressed his belief that God has a first and second choice for each life. Happy are those individuals who get in on His first, His best, plan. Those who fail often have to settle for next, or second, best. This may not be altogether bad, but nothing can replace the satisfaction His first choice brings.

"I can still get in on God's first will for my life," Buddy exclaimed joyfully. "I'm a little late getting started, but there's still time."

"And I'll do all I can to help you," I promised, bubbling with excitement. This was a dream come true for me, too. All my life I had dreamed of being a preacher's wife. Like Ma.

That afternoon God's call came to my husband with such force and blessing that every doubt was erased. From that day to this he has never again questioned his divine appointment. Many discouragements have come to disquiet and disturb him, but one thing has remained invariable. His confrontation with God in the upper room of our little gray house on Richfield Road cinched forever his call to the ministry. That was another miracle. Many more were to follow.

3

Getting Started

Naturally a call to preach is also a call to prepare. And that can be a challenge if a family is involved. Getting my husband educated was asking for more than one miracle. To start with, I needed a job while he was in college. Second, we needed a place to live. And following so close on the heels of World War II, housing was almost nonexistent and sky-high.

"I'll work at anything," I had promised eagerly. "I'll take a job in a dime store if necessary."

Then out of the blue an idea dawned on me. Because of the recent global conflict and the transference of many educators to industry, special certification was being offered to former teachers, enticing them to return to the schoolroom. Was it possible that I, too, could obtain a "Special"? If so, that would take care of the bread and butter. And there might be enough left over for some jam or jelly. Or, peanut butter. (And to think I had resented Dad's insistence that I become a teacher! Now I can plainly see it was all a part of God's plan for our lives.)

Fairly bursting with excitement, I could scarcely wait for Buddy's nightly call from the shop.

"Honey, I've got a tremendous idea!" I exploded when at long last the telephone rang.

"Well, let's hear it," he urged amiably from the other end of the line. His call home during lunch break gave him a brief reprieve from the factory grind.

"Maybe it's too much to hope for," I demurred, "but do you think there's the slightest chance I could teach while you go to school next year?"

"You mean, get a special certificate?"

"I was offered a school some time back, wasn't I? If I could have gotten a 'Special' then, couldn't I get one now?"

"I don't see why not."

"We could give it a try."

"That would really be the answer, wouldn't it?"

We had been praying for guidance about the school Buddy should attend. One college we were considering was located in a nice town 30 miles west of us. It was not as large or influential as a second one in another state. But it offered a good spiritual and academic program and would give him the theological training he needed. Furthermore, the transition would be much simpler and easier to make.

"If you could get a teaching job, the matter of choosing a college would be automatically settled," Buddy said.

"Then we only would have to find a place to rent."

"Right! I don't intend to buy another house!" he said emphatically.

Not long after, we bundled up the children and made a trip to the county seat of the area in which the nearer college was located.

Although slim blades of green slashed their way up through the damp, dark earth, and daffodils and tulips spotted the drab landscape with color, the air was unusually crisp and sharp. The vicious wind bit deep into our flesh, stinging the marrow of our bones.

Little Sue had the mumps, so Daddy stayed in the warm car with the girls while I, stiff with apprehension, approached the imposing stone building and entered the office.

Unfortunately the county superintendent of schools was out for the day. Nevertheless her office girl asked me to leave my name, qualifications, and telephone number.

"We'll have to come back again," I told Buddy as I sat in the car, feeling both disappointed and hopeful. "Mrs. Smith wasn't in the office today."

"What are your chances? Have any idea?"

"Her secretary asked me to return. Sounds pretty good."

A few days later I received a call from the office of the county superintendent of schools. The superintendent herself was speaking. She had received my application; and would I be interested in interviewing a school board? The school was located just outside the town in which the college was located.

Would I?

An appointment was made. The interview proved successful. A contract was signed in no time at all. Our feet scarcely touched the ground. How thrilling! The Lord was leading! He had worked another miracle in our behalf!

*   *   *

But what about a place to live?

That proved to be a far greater challenge.

Saturday after Saturday we tucked the girls in the backseat and made the tiresome jaunt, searching for a house to rent. Invariably we returned home weary, hungry, and disappointed.

After Buddy had gone to work one afternoon, I was washing the dishes and praying earnestly as I worked. "O Lord, You know we have looked and looked, and we cannot find a house or an apartment anywhere. Please help us find a place to live."

"Buy a house with a small down payment. You can afford a $200 or $300 investment after you have sold this place and paid your bills," a voice whispered.

But this suggestion can't be coming from the Lord, I thought. It was absolutely impossible to buy a house anywhere with such a small down payment.

"Buy a house with a small down payment!" The startling impression came the second time. Again, clearly and distinctly.

Just in case it was the Holy Spirit, I prayed, "But You know Buddy declares he will not buy another house . . . and when he makes up his mind . . ."

Yet again came the message with unmistakable clarity: *"Buy a house with a small down payment."*

Remembering Gideon, I continued, "If this message is from You, Lord, direct us to the right house—the one You have for us. And change Buddy's mind about buying."

On another exhausting house-hunting expedition we once again failed to find anything, and we were discouraged.

"Remember that first real estate office we tried?" I asked. "It's been quite some time since we were there. Perhaps the agent has something by now. Let's give it one more try."

To my astonishment Buddy replied, "What street was that on?"

"It's in this area—somewhere near here. I think you turned too soon."

Bringing the car to halt on a maple-lined street, he intended to back up and proceed eastward.

"There's a house for sale!" I exclaimed excitedly. "Right here. On my side of the street. Isn't it a cute place?"

Buddy bent forward to look at the white house with blue shutters. "It is for sale, isn't it? But it's pretty small."

"It would be large enough for us."

"They're probably asking far more than we could afford. It's practically brand-new."

"We could ask about it."

"I guess there would be no harm in asking. Where do you suppose we could find out about it?"

"What about the house next door?" I asked, looking askance at my husband. "You said you wouldn't buy a house under any circumstances."

"Let's take a look, anyway."

Just as I should have expected, God had gone before. Buddy discovered that the owners lived in the very house where he had gone to inquire. Returning to the car, he said, "Come on. She is going to show it to us."

"My two sons built this as sort of an investment after they returned from the service," the graying woman explained.

We walked slowly through the place, admiring it—silently.

"How much are they asking for it?" Buddy finally ventured to ask.

"They have been holding out for $7,000," she replied. "They want $1,000 down. But they might take less. They need the money and are anxious to get it off their hands."

We looked the house over again—more admiringly this time. The nice-sized living room was paneled attractively. There was a dining area between it and the kitchen, a full bath, two bedrooms, and a basement with a furnace. And it was clean and ready for occupancy.

Back in the car once again we expressed our approval. "And look, there's a school right next door. Sybil would have only a few steps to go to school each day."

"I think I'll make them an offer," Buddy declared after a bit.

Somehow I refrained from remarking, "But I thought . . ." I was thinking, instead, of that message I had received while washing the dishes that day: *Buy a house with a small down payment.*

Moments later Buddy returned. Without speaking he started the engine.

When I could stand it no longer, I asked, "Well, what about it?"

"They will take $5,000," he replied, fairly bursting with pleasure.

"Five thousand! The house is only two years old! Why, the lady said it cost more than that to build!" It was incredible! Unbelievable! Even for those preinflation days!

"I offered to give them a small down payment—$200 or $300."

"You don't mean it!"

"They're going to think about it and call us. I'm sure we'll hear from them in a few days."

"What a miracle that would be!"

"In the meantime we must pray about it."

But I already had.

Four weeks later we moved into 708 South Park Street, just a few blocks from the college where Buddy would attend, two or three miles from the rural school I would teach, and next door to the one our little girl would attend. We had purchased the white house with blue shutters for $5,000, a down payment of $200, and monthly payments less than we would have expended for rent.

With a livelihood provided for and a house in which to live, my husband was ready to begin making preparations for his great adventure in the ministry.

Our cup was full and running over.

4

Rookies

My husband had been in school only a short time when his feet began to itch. Like many another apprentice, he became impatient to practice his trade. Accordingly, he inquired about taking a student pastorate. His previous evangelistic experience and our music served as effective enticements. Soon he received a call to pastor a small congregation, the one his superintendent called "the fightingest church" on his district.

Besides the obvious challenge, Assignment 1 meant making at least three 60-mile trips a week—through snow and blow, rain and sleet, as well as balmy weather. It also involved getting sleepy children into pajamas and tucked into bed when we arrived home late on Sunday and Wednesday evenings.

"This one thing I can promise you," Buddy told his overseer, "if I can't help a church, I shall do my best not to hurt it." And that was his philosophy for as long as he pastored.

Fortunately, Buddy was endowed with a talent for helping churches that were hurting or had been wounded. While God has given some men the gift to hew out new congregations or build fine edifices, He gave my husband the unique ability to apply healing balm, help resolve conflicts, and unite feuding factions. This faculty was to prove strong in his behalf—from the very beginning of his ministry.

A first pastorate is one you never forget—for at least one or more reasons. We especially remember ours because we loved and were loved by both sides.

Rookies begin any profession with gilded aspirations, anticipating the good, not the bad. Promotion, not demotion. But disappointments, adversities, and conflicts invariably come in the due process of time.

This applies to eager, starry-eyed preachers as well as ballplayers or policemen. Doing God's will brings fulfillment and happiness. Yet it is unrealistic to anticipate only rose blossoms. Serving in the ministry involves some thorny stickers (and a few stinkers), also. However, no victory is achieved, no miracle received, without first overcoming a challenge.

We learned very early that it isn't easy to be caught between opposing forces, to have two factions vying for your support and approbation. In this case a couple of older women (we scarcely had any men) headed the sparring teams.

I must confess I leaned a bit toward Bertha's corner. She disliked her rival's ways and means of exercising control, but from my vantage point, it seemed she threw fewer punches and exhibited better sportsmanship than Beulah. Besides, she wasn't jealous of me. However, we also spent less time in her home than we did in her opponent's.

Beulah's Ben had built their primitive house far back from the road at the end of a long lane on the edge of the woods, using tree limbs for rafters. The dining room floor was so uneven it called for cautious preambulation. At night oil lamps cast eerie shadows on the stained ceiling and walls, while a wood-burning heater failed to adequately ward off the winter drafts. But we enjoyed going there. Beulah and Ben were content in their little world. Their talk was jocular. Their laughter, rollicking. Our frequent visits were jovial affairs.

While Ben bragged about the squash he raised and the berries he picked, Beulah gloated over her baking, the years she had served as Sunday School superintendent in a church of another denomination, and her Irish wit. Despite her sharp and pungent jabs at Bertha and me, we still found her caustic tongue amusing.

Because Beulah and Ben had no means of transportation, except for his horse and homemade cart, it became a part of our pastoral duty to convey them to and from the church services. To show their appreciation they frequently invited us to share their meager board, which consisted mainly of potatoes, winter squash, an occasional roast, and the luscious bread Beulah expertly produced in her lean-to kitchen. Some of the wild blackberries Ben gathered in the summertime went into mouth-watering cobblers. Others helped fill jam and jelly jars.

We enjoyed the hospitality Beulah and Ben offered us. We also appreciated their contributions to our larder, although it didn't take long to recognize that remuneration was expected by way of public praise and approbation.

One thing was decidedly clear: Beulah wanted to be the Sunday School superintendent. And it didn't take her long to begin campaigning—for Bertha's job. Not only did Beulah covet her opponent's position, but she was envious of me, too. Wasn't I closer to the pastor than any other person?

That Beulah favored my husband was all too apparent.

"Nothing is too good for my pastor," she would say, quickly and cunningly clasping a hand over her mouth. Muffling forced laughter, she declared roguishly, "I love my pastor."

An extremely proud, rather pretty lady despite her questionable age, Beulah always appeared in public, primped and powdered, looking well preserved. But her amply padded frame made it very difficult for her to climb in and out of the backseat of our two-door sedan. Also, she longed to share the front seat with the driver. This she made known with count-less hints and pithy asides, always accompanied by the same stifled laughter.

For months the Lord enabled me to take her "insulated" but insinuating blows in good grace. And with humor. Finally, she came into her glory when we changed automobiles and I was forced into the backseat because she could not possibly manipulate the crawl space.

"We've got her out of the way now, haven't we?" she crooned, sitting very straight and importantly next to "her preacher."

Although my husband was always the gentleman, and Beulah was old enough to be his mother—or grandmother—still her undisguised partiality created a lump in my throat that was hard to swallow. Her jealous digs and verbal slaps stung keenly.

To add fuel to the fire, I often arrived at church on the verge of exhaustion. I was teaching in a demanding situation so "her preacher" could go to school and pastor her church, which paid little more than traveling expenses. In addition to my hours in the classroom, there was housework to do, a husband and children to care for, and night classes to attend. Still, she persistently hurled arrows in my direction—under the guise of witticisms. Even her gifts were directed more to my husband than to me.

"Nothing is too good for my pastor," she insisted.

The height of her ridiculous actions was reached on the last day of our stay in that assignment, but more about that a bit later on.

*   *   *

Ben was a character in his own right. Though in his 70s, he was tall, straight, loud-talking, bighearted, and weak-willed. He loved to raise squash and pick wild blackberries. He loved to sing, too. During the intervals when he was in right relationship with the Lord, he would stand up in church—work clothes, knee boots, galluses, et al.—and warble his heart out.

But Ben loved to play cards, smoke on the side, and nip occasionally. And all these things were contrary to the church rules.

Ben followed up his frequent digressions with a trip to the public altar, repenting tearfully, and making his confession openly and freely. But his spurts of reform never lasted long.

"Ben was down at the beer garden again this week. His horse was tied to the hitching post out front."

This was the usual story. We heard it frequently when arriving for services.

"Ben is in the beer garden again," someone informed us on a Wednesday night.

"Let's go in and get him out," Buddy said, ready for action. He had persistently minimized the complaints, but enough was enough. At long last it was time to take the bull by the horns.

Sure enough, there in the smoke-filled din, at the front table with three other men sat Ben, hat askew, cigarette dangling from the corner of his mouth, holding a deck of cards. A mug of beer frothed close by.

"Ben, will you come outside with me?" my husband asked, not unkindly.

"Yes, sir, Brother Spray!" Ben replied jovially.

Out on the sidewalk Buddy told Ben he could no longer belong to the church.

"Oh, that's all right, Brother Spray, I understand."

"I'm sorry to have to do this . . ."

"Oh, it's all right."

"We're still friends?"

"Why, shore! I don't blame you one bit!"

After that Ben remained just as friendly as ever, but he began smoking openly, indulging his sinful habits in such a heady, I-could-care-less manner that he resembled a rebellious teenager.

When we went to church on a Sunday morning a few months later, we were met at the door by a group of sad people.

"Ben died last night," they cried.

"What?"

"Ben died last night. He had a heart attack."

That week Buddy stood at the head of an open grave and spoke those mournful words: " 'We have come now to commit the body of our departed friend to its kindred dust. . . .' "

Thus, in a quiet country cemetery, amid towering, rugged oaks, my husband consigned Ben's body back to the earth from whence it had come. It was the first of many committals that were to follow.

*　　*　　*

On a happier note, Assignment 1 also brought Buddy his first wedding, one we recall with chuckles.

The spanking new preacher, reveling in his vernal importance, performed the ceremony without a hitch. " 'I pronounce that they are husband and wife together, in the name of the Father, and of the Son, and of the Holy Spirit. Those whom God has joined together let no man put asunder,' " he declared solemnly and authoritatively.

Then, following the recessional, Buddy waited expectantly while the photographer assembled the wedding party and began snapping pictures. But no one gave him a second glance, his newly acquired checkered bow tie notwithstanding. (It now reposes in a trunk with other keepsakes. And, by the way, Buddy eventually learned to dress more conservatively when performing rituals.)

Eventually the photographer realized he had overlooked the clergyman. Approaching the preacher, he confessed with chagrin, "I'm sorry. I thought you were the groom or one of his attendants."

*   *   *

When time came to leave Assignment 1, it was not without some pulling on the heartstrings. And I might add, this was to be so true of each subsequent assignment, also.

"Stay. Please stay with us," the people urged tearfully.

"But you aren't able to support us," my husband insisted. We knew we could not exist on the salary they were paying when I stopped teaching and returned to being a full-time homemaker.

"You'd be surprised what we could do," they cried.

Nevertheless, we felt it wise to move on. I was suffering from exhaustion. Besides, God's will includes making exits as well as entrances. Closing a door on the present at the proper time is as important as entering a portal when God beckons.

*   *   *

Beulah had invited us to her house for dinner following the morning service on our final day.

"Rev. Spray," she said, after we had driven into the yard and were getting out of the car, "I'd like to speak to you in private. Let's step over here."

What's so important that she can't share it with me, too? I wondered as she impressively maneuvered "her preacher" aside, completely snubbing the little girls and me.

Later on in the day when we had a few moments alone, my husband confided, "It was nothing she couldn't have told you, too. It has to do with the evening service."

That night Beulah proudly strode to the platform. "I would like for Brother Spray to step forward," she announced, again completely ignoring me. "Rev. Spray, we want you to know how sorry we are to lose you. We have

41

appreciated your ministry so much. Some friends of yours have taken up an offering, and we would like to present it to you at this time."

Once more the grace of God enabled me to smile. But the scales were favorably balanced, or at least tipped, when in the same service Bertha distinctly included us both when she presented us with additional gifts.

One, a beautiful quilt, represented many hours of labor by the church women. Each block bore the embroidered names of a church family; the whole quilt included not just a certain few, but members and friends of both factions.

Despite Beulah's countless unnecessary and stinging jabs, the Lord kept me sweet and helped me to remain silent and harbor no resentment; and someday I hope to see her in heaven. Not that her punches didn't hurt, but love does "cover the multitude of sins" (1 Pet. 4:8). That is a miracle in itself.

I must confess that Beulah was not the only person in that church to get her back up against the preacher's wife, however. Mrs. Klein had her eye on a certain job, too, and when I nominated another person, she refused to speak to me for weeks, nor shake hands.

"Good morning, Mrs. Klein," I'd say. When she failed to extend her hand, I reached out, lifted it up, and shook it amiably. Not once but many times. And persistency paid off. Shortly after we had left the church, we received a letter from this lady. "For all the things I've said against you and Brother Spray," she wrote, "I pray you'll forgive."

We learned early that it pays to go the second mile, to turn the other cheek, when problems arise in the church. I confess I have asked forgiveness when I truly believe it was unnecessary, but I chose to swallow my pride because I did not want to be responsible for another's harm or hurt. Fortunately, there are no calories in eating humble pie.

*　　*　　*

Assignment 1 was not without its challenges, especially for a couple of rookies. But miraculously the church prospered. The attendance increased. The factions held together. And we left retaining many happy, and some sad, memories of "the fightingest church" on that superintendent's district.

5

Assignment 2

Moving into the parsonage was a feat in itself—to say nothing of the events which followed in Assignment 2.

The former occupants had closed the parsonage door, locked it, and taken up lodging elsewhere, leaving most of their possessions inside. This made it impossible (supposedly) for the incoming pastor (us) to take up residency.

But something had to be done! After selling our house on South Park Street several weeks earlier, we were obligated to turn over the keys to the new owner. And since my husband had been officially hired, he was expected to assume the pastoral duties of this charge.

Finally we decided to move into the parsonage, our predecessor's belongings notwithstanding. And that's what we did. But not without some tension.

The parsonage was old and huge. Since there were four bedrooms on the second floor, we decided to put all of the upstairs' furnishings into the unusually large middle room. Everything belonging to the former occupants, including curtains and window fixtures, went into that space.

This state of affairs, I must say, did not promote the cheeriest, most relaxing, sleep-inducing atmosphere, especially for the children. In *Daily Delights* I told about the first night.

"I don't think we're going to be happy here," Sybil sobbed.

"Oh yes, Honey, we shall," I promised, assuming a bravado I certainly did not feel. "We shall be happy here just like we have been happy everywhere else we have lived."

That was, in truth, the "substance of things hoped for," not "the evidence of things" seen (Heb. 11:1).

Downstairs we used the front room and woodshed in which to store the remainder of the goods belonging to our predecessors. Then arranging our own furniture the best way we could, we settled down for a long autumn's wait—without any napping.

Since the former occupants retained a key to the house, we never knew when they might walk in. One day we returned from a drive to find a note on our kitchen door. It informed us these folks would move their possessions as soon as the church paid them the week's salary they had coming.

Evidently they did not realize we were living in the parsonage because there was an additional message penned on the envelope: "Please nail the back door shut when you get your things in."

Five weeks of constant stress and strain took an extravagant toll of my physical strength. When my legs began turning black and blue, the church board decided to take action.

A lawyer was consulted. He informed the former occupants that legal action would be taken against them unless they moved their possessions out of the parsonage.

Following a prayer meeting service soon after, we discovered a truck backed up to our front door when we emerged from the church. My husband approached the former pastor, extended his hand, and told him his name.

Disregarding Buddy's overture of friendship, the disenchanted preacher proceeded to load the truck with as many pieces of furniture as it would hold. Then he drove away, leaving the residue behind.

Again we were in a quandary.

Another decision had to be made. What were we to do now? At last we decided to transfer the leftovers to the woodshed. Some weeks later, relatives came and salvaged what they wanted. The leavings were left to our disposal. Years later, my accumulation of Christmas materials still contains program books which once belonged to that pastor's wife.

*   *   *

It didn't take long, nevertheless, to recognize that not all the ailments of that assignment were due to outside forces. There was an inside job with which to cope, too. We soon learned that that problem was embodied in another strong personality.

Each Sunday morning Edgar stealthfully crept into the sanctuary, clutching his Bible tightly to his side. But his countenance did not mirror the Good News proclaimed therein. He exuded no inner joy. In fact, his face was about as solemn as Big Ben's on a rainy day in London.

"We need to carry a burden," he urged the people repeatedly. This was the theme of his religion, one his visage clearly promulgated. Certainly we agreed that Christians should be concerned, deeply concerned, about the unsaved and the welfare of those in need. But Jesus said our prayer and fasting should be done in secret. He has bid us cast all our cares on Him so we can give the world our smiles. Edgar evidently overlooked this in his struggle for recognition and his yen for power.

Actually we found it amusing the way this man responded when monetary pledges were taken. If his name received notice and the amount of his giving was made public, he gave liberally. On the other hand, if secret pledges were received, you could count him out of the almsgiving.

"What we need is a leader," he declared Sunday after Sunday. What he really meant, of course, was "What this church needs is me for its leader!"

And our frustration increased. Once a parishioner grew bold and told him, "Brother Edgar, we have a leader. All we need to do is follow him." But her suggestion was ignored.

Time brought no lessening of pressure. Because Edgar taught an adult Sunday School class, he had a captive audience regularly. "What we need is a leader," he vociferated week after week.

Finally out of desperation we sought the advice of an older person, a longtime minister, a godly individual who was well acquainted with handling personality conflicts within congregations.

"Pray him out," the minister told us. "That's what I had to do." The tale of woe we heard that day matched ours to a tee, releasing us from all personal guilt.

"I'm going upstairs to pray," I told my husband not long after that visit. I had fixed dinner and put it on the table. It was Sunday and the usual incantations had been heard again. "You and the girls go ahead and eat. I can't take this anymore."

Upstairs by the furnace register in the gray and rose-papered bedroom, I unloaded my burden to the Lord. The Good Shepherd had put us in charge of this flock. He knew how to deal with a troublesome sheep. He cared for Edgar. He cared for us. And He knew exactly how to solve the problem.

After some time in prayer, the load I had been carrying was lifted. Assurance came. The Lord would take care of it all. I knew that beyond any shadow of a doubt. My heaviness vanished. Joy and hope took its place.

By Tuesday my husband was feeling exactly like I had felt after coming home from church on Sunday. "I'm going over to the church to pray," he said. When he returned, his load had been lifted, too.

Very early the next morning the telephone rang and I answered it.

"That was Doris," I told Buddy. "Brother Edgar is in the hospital and not expected to live."

"Really?"

"No kidding!"

"What's the trouble?"

"They don't know, but he's in Mercy Hospital."

"Not expected to live?" Buddy asked in disbelief.

"That's what Doris said."

When we arrived at the hospital, an impenetrable curtain of gloom hung over the man's room. The atmosphere was saturated with darkness and oppression. Hostility glowered heavily, so heavily we hesitated to step over the threshold. The poor nurses felt it, too, and were anxious and frustrated by his raucousness.

"I've come to pray for you," my husband began.

"Do you think the Lord will hear you?" Edgar asked belligerently.

After weeks of suffering and hospitalization, he recovered and returned to church, but Edgar was not the same. His prestige and power were gone and, as far as I know, never returned. Although a former pastor had "prayed him out," we were only successful in "praying him down." But that was enough, for he caused us no trouble thereafter.

I'll confess I have wondered why God allowed this man to live when he was so close to death. Perhaps in His infinite mercy God saw fit to give him a second chance. If so, I sincerely hope Edgar took advantage of it and we meet him again someday in heaven.

I do know that God answered our prayers. And answered prayer is always a miracle. Furthermore, through it all we learned very early in our ministry that the Lord can handle any situation—and the most difficult people—if we commit the problem to Him. Again, to Him be the glory!

*   *   *

From its earliest years, Assignment 2 had been known for some of its straitlaced, radical members. Despite the consistent Spirit-filled Christians who devotedly served the Lord and gave us their loyal support, a few created tensions by trying to thrust their ideas on others.

I'll never forget the day Sadie hobbled into the parsonage to speak her mind. One of her complaints centered around the evils of the relatively new medium of television. (If she thought it was bad then, what would she think now?)

We had purchased our first set a few months earlier. For quite some time we kept our one-eyed monster in the large room upstairs. When we waxed bold enough, we moved it downstairs into the front room where it reposed at that very moment, although I am very sure Sadie had not seen it because of her failing eyesight. Or she may have been seated with her back to it. From my vantage point in the dining room where I was ironing, I could not tell.

My husband, nevertheless, was stationed in the wide doorway between the two of us where he could observe us both. From where she sat, Sadie could not see me, just as I could not see her from my position. On and on she chattered like a magpie, venting her opinions to her pastor, while I convulsed with suppressed laughter.

Buddy's phlegmatic nature proved a genuine asset that day. He listened respectfully and attentively to her, watched me as I doubled up with stifled mirth, and maintained an expressionless face through it all. Call it what you may, but I think that, too, was a miracle.

Willard was a snappy-dressing bachelor in his 70s. Despite the fact that he was somewhat of a fashion plate himself, he repeatedly denounced women's dress. Finally, when his rabid comments threatened to drive away our young people, my husband was forced to reprove him. When Buddy asked him bluntly just how long he thought women's dresses should be, Willard replied, "Six inches from the floor," and that was long before daytime "maxi" wear. And, although he wore gold-rimmed glasses himself, Willard strongly denounced wedding rings and the wearing of gold.

By this time we had been married a goodly number of years, but I had never had a wedding ring. Feeling the need for one at long last, we made a trip to the big city where we purchased a plain band for $6.00. After we got back home, however, both of us had some second thoughts. For one thing, what would the dogmatists (this included Willard) do and say when they saw a gold band on my finger?

A short time later I received my answer—and it came straight from heaven while I was standing before the refrigerator in the kitchen. *Put on your wedding ring, and I will take care of the people.*

Grandma Jones had ruled the church and pastors for years with an iron hand and sharp tongue. Before entering the local convalescent home where we held services regularly, she had considered it her duty, so we were told, to visit the parsonage early in the morning to make certain the pastor was out of bed. Now I, too, was in dread of her. What would she say when she saw my hand?

Put on your wedding ring, and I'll take care of the people. The message had been clear and definite. So I put on my simple band and God kept His word. Grandma Jones glared but uttered not a syllable. Nor did anyone else.

* * *

If it seems that our first two assignments were real stumpers, they were. I believe I am not exaggerating when I say that even for veteran preachers, these churches would have been hefty challenges to their ingenuity and spiritual stamina.

Certainly we made mistakes. Aren't all novices entitled to that privilege? But we were sincere and we diligently tried to excel. Fortunately, the Lord helped us (both in those earliest years and the ones to follow) despite our errors in judgment.

For years I lived in anticipation of finding the perfect pastorate. After several disappointments, I accepted the fact that wherever people are, there are going to be problems. However, our God is able and willing to meet our needs, whatever they are.

Assignment 2, nevertheless, brought many spiritual victories and gave us precious memories. Friendships were established which last to this day.

*   *   *

"I'm afraid I'm going to lose that church," our superintendent had told his superior before Buddy accepted the assignment.

"If it goes, it goes," the general replied.

But the church did not take on water and sink as our leader feared. It recouped its resources and grew in numbers under my husband's leadership.

Today a beautiful edifice houses a congregation in that once sleepy town, and God's work moves forward. How thrilling to know we had a part in the rescue and resuscitation of that drowning congregation! Again, to God be the glory! He is the Worker of miracles.

6

Assignment 3

After we had decided to leave Assignment 2, a delegation from a larger congregation came to worship with us one Sunday evening. Following the service these men openly voiced their approval of what they had seen and heard, promising we would hear from them shortly.

Becoming pastor of their church would be a substantial promotion and we lived expectantly for weeks. But no news was forthcoming. Following what seemed an eternity, we finally learned that they had kept their word. They had asked for my husband but met with opposition from a higher level. (Years later they got what they had asked for earlier, and we enjoyed a rewarding ministry with this friendly group.)

But why was their earlier request turned down? Perhaps a step-up just then for Buddy would have invoked the displeasure of more experienced men. Or perhaps God knew he wasn't ready for the challenge. Whatever, our superintendent found it most difficult to inform us of the negative decision.

That was our first real disappointment in the ministry. We felt it—naturally. Nonetheless, it caused us to learn early to "pray through" our hurts and keep a sanctified spirit.

"That's all right," Buddy assured Dr. Deen, without a trace of rancor. "We are prepared to accept the decision. We have sincerely prayed for God's will to be done. We believe this is it. So please don't feel badly about it."

Evidently this towering gentleman had not anticipated that response. His eyes filled with tears and astonishment. With great warmth he expressed both his regret for our thwarted hopes and his appreciation for our attitude.

The hardest part for me was not the disappointment. It was the move to the next place which Buddy accepted sight unseen.

* * *

To get to Assignment 3 you followed the main street of town across the railroad tracks to the grain elevator, which stood on one corner, and a dilapidated monstrosity of a house, on another. There you turned off on a muddy side street, passed through a marshy bog, over the creek, and onward. At the end of the road crouched a low, cracked, cement block structure which strongly resembled both a blacksmith shop and a rural grocery store-gas station. That, the home-made sign said, was my husband's new stomping ground.

Next door, a former barracks building, purchased from the government for a pittance and remodeled, served as the parsonage. It was slightly larger than a cracker box and almost as flimsy.

Our first Sunday came on the heels of my ·husband's ordination, the culmination of hopes, dreams, and years of study. The induction service on the preceding Thursday evening had been the high point of our lives. I shall never forget the tears that ran unrestrained down the face of one particular elder as he observed our moment of triumph. Nor can I forget the gentle squeeze my husband gave me at the conclusion of the ceremonies. It was a time of mutual closeness, both to each other and to God.

We had endeavored to make this event an exciting, exultant experience for the girls, too. Dressed in new skirts (blue for Sybil and pink for Sue) and lace-trimmed blouses, they sat on the front row, giving rapt attention. (Perhaps that was when Sybil's persistent urge to be a minister's wife was conceived. Who knows?)

The candidates' wives were presented with lovely corsages, and for some unknown reason, my husband and I were chosen to lead the procession. The evening was one of celebration and promise, but our elation was destined for short duration. Our bubble burst in a hurry when we got our first glimpse of Assignment 3 the following Sunday morning.

We drove up (we had not moved our belongings yet) to "possess the land" in our new blue-green Ford. If I could have foreseen the woebegone situation that awaited us, I might not have dressed so carefully. My navy sheer, white gloves, and ordination corsage seemed decidedly out of place, I soon discovered.

But the message the presiding general superintendent had issued on Thursday evening could not have been more apropos.

"Remember, ladies," he had admonished, "there is no defense against love."

That is the admonition I have endeavored to live by ever since—from that disconcerting day to this.

"'Lo, folks," Katrina said in a thick brogue, thrusting a lesson leaflet at us as we entered one of the most unattractive auditoriums imaginable.

The Celotex on the low ceiling was faded and dirty. Some of the woodwork had been originally varnished. Part had been painted white. The portions that were visible through the myrid of posters and printed miscellany suggested that the walls had once been peach-colored. Now they were ugly, faded, and in need of more paint.

A green chalkboard dominated the space between the two bare windows on the west wall. On the opposite side of the room, along with taped-up messages, a lonely clothes hanger hung askew.

Behind the pulpit, surrounding a goodly sized Sallman's *Head of Christ*, flapping letters spelled out "LO, I AM WITH YOU ALWAY."

A bit to the left of center on the front wall, a Cradle Roll display dangled beside the door. Miniature cradles, bearing the names of the congregation's young, glued on lengths of blue and pink ribbon, trailed from the larger cradle at the top.

A rack for hats and coats stood at the back of the room. And sitting beside the oil-burning stove was Grandpa Holloway. This was the spot he claimed summer and winter, unbathed body, unlaundered clothing, and smelly boots notwithstanding.

Rows of folding chairs filled the room. And added to the crowded visage were two unnecessary plant stands. Stationed on either side of the pulpit before the altar, they scarcely allowed room for one to get to the platform.

Our first job was unmistakably clear. We didn't have to spend days in fasting and prayer for guidance. This message blazed at us in fluorescent rays: *Do something about the sanctuary immediately!*

This we set about to do with the help of willing workers as soon as possible. Down came the flapping letters, the taped-up messages, and the coat hanger. Down came the Cradle Roll roster from the front wall, and up it went at the back of the room. On went new paint. And out went the flower stands.

Our second challenge involved encouraging and helping various members of the congregation. A humble lot, these people, for the most part, subsisted on low incomes, but they were loving, eager to please, and sacrificial. Because of their big hearts and willingness to give, they had been bled financially until they were lacking in many of life's necessities— dental attention, eyeglasses, clothing, and household wares.

What a thrill it was to observe the change that came over them! Our recognition and praise met with sincere appre-

55

ciation. One by one, these people acquired a new look and a new outlook, as well. They literally blossomed—like fruit trees warmed by an early spring sun.

But the metamorphosis did not take place instantaneously, and I must confess that the first six months were very disheartening ones. During this time I kept the venetian blinds closed in our living room so I could not see the church building.

Each Sunday morning when I dressed for church, I would ask myself, "How would I dress if I were going to First Church today?" It helped boost my own morale, and hopefully, it served to inspire others.

Our third challenge had to do with finances. Included in our pastoral inheritance were embarrassing unpaid obligations. In time the Lord enabled us to face the world with a clear conscience. All bills were paid in full and eventually the church was operating in the black.

Despite the humble circumstances (or perhaps because of them), God's presence moved among us in a special way in our services. When it came to praying, no other congregation ever equaled this one in the matter of intercession. Wonderful times of victory were shared around the altar.

Brother Wallace was an especially spiritual man who often spoke affectionately of his "problem God." Moreover, his talks with the Heavenly Father caused heaven and earth to join hands.

When the basement flooded, as it did frequently, seven or eight classes were forced to meet in the one-room auditorium. Need I add, bedlam prevailed. However, people continued to come.

At times our crowds were so large every seat was taken, with standing room only. This was especially true of our monthly singspiration services when we placed no restriction on talent. Anyone who wanted to participate was free to do so. Whenever I hear the song "Balm in Gilead," I am reminded with a grin of the fellow who sang it, flatting out each time on "Gilead."

Our mandolin and guitar bore coveted spots on the program, as did Amy's accordion. Even Victor's mouth organ was appreciated.

Quartets, duets, solos—good, bad, or indifferent—when combined with the instrumental numbers served to draw crowds and create enthusiasm.

And there were fun times, too! I doubt if the people who were teens at the time will ever forget the box social held in the tiny parsonage. For entertainment the young people got down on their knees to put jigsaw puzzles together on the floor.

My favorite recollection has to do with one of our wedding anniversaries. The Millers had invited us to their home for the evening meal, which included a pretty anniversary cake and all the trimmings. Before we could get away from the sumptuous table, the church people began coming in. Later, Rev. Scott, a retired minister, arrived, but we thought little about that as he occasionally visited our church.

The fun really began when the ladies cunningly enticed me into the back bedroom. There they began preparing me for the mock wedding they had planned with great secrecy.

Someone had made a gown out of an old sheet and overlaid it with coarse netting. The open front was secured with huge safety pins. The belt, a wide sash of pink crepe paper, sported a large bow in the back. Next came the veil with its tiara of shirred lace, centered with a pink crepe paper rose. My bouquet consisted of various household brushes and aged artificial flowers, tied with a large blue ribbon.

Since several of the men worked at the local foundry, piston rings, carefully gilted, were used for wedding bands. They were borne on a large bed pillow by one of the fellows who was small of stature. His plump, smiling wife carried my train. The man with the "problem God" acted as father of the bride, and I entered on his arm. After he gave me away, Rev. Scott "married" us, using a large magazine for a wedding manual.

Following the ceremony, a table loaded down with gifts—towels, tablecloths, sheets, pillowcases, a rug, a skillet, a bedspread, place mats, and other miscellaneous items— was brought out. We are still using some of those items well over a quarter of a century later.

Climaxing it all, a huge wedding cake, complete with miniature bride and groom, ice cream slices centered with pink wedding bells, and engraved napkins were produced as if by magic.

The effect was overwhelming. We had not received the slightest inkling of what was going on. (Years later we would learn just how quietly a congregation can carry on behind a pastor's back—in quite a different way.) Usually my intuition or imagination gives with a few surmises, but not that time.

No group before or since has excelled this one in remembering the parsonage family on birthdays, Christmases, and anniversaries. They truly made us feel loved and wanted. My husband looked on that portion of his ministry as his happiest for many years following.

Despite the depths to which we were plunged upon arriving, God proved strong in our behalf and worked many miracles during our stay in Assignment 3—just as He would continue to do in the years yet to come.

7

Assignment 4

At first Assignment 4 was a greater challenge for my husband than it was for me, despite my aversion to moving into another pint-sized parsonage. Hadn't we lived in cramped quarters long enough? This house was slightly, if any, larger than the last one. However, I loved moving to the city.

Buddy found it more difficult to adjust to urban living. Furthermore, both the church and parsonage had been constructed on a former city dump. Passing trucks jarred the shifting earth, causing dishes and windows to rattle—and sensitive nerves to jangle. Adjusting to the unsettling living conditions was not easy, but my husband soon learned he was faced with a second problem which necessitated immediate attention.

The church was practically dying on the vine. For a time it appeared that the entire congregation would die physically as well.

"It looks like everyone waited for us to get here so I could bury them," Buddy remarked a bit dispiritedly. Since his predecessor had been in poor health and declined to officiate at funerals, one almost wondered if Buddy's observation held some logic. Immediately he was kept busy burying the dead—and the size of the congregation was limited to begin with.

In spite of the morbid send-off, the Spirit of the Lord began moving on the troubled waters, reviving, renewing, and healing. The upbeat messages my husband brought Sunday after Sunday were received hungrily. Many years later a member of this congregation would tell him, "We always thought of you as our love pastor. If it hadn't been for you, Daddy would not have died in such good victory as he did."

Throughout that assignment funerals continued to come, but fortunately they came with less frequency after the initiation period. Perhaps the Lord was preparing Buddy for what was to follow. During the subsequent years of his ministry, he has offered comfort and consolation to a host of mourners, officiating at many funerals—for both young and old. There have been graveside services for newborn infants and the funeral service ("Make it short," the family requested) for one 104-year-old grandmother who remembered hearing Abraham Lincoln speak during his presidential campaign. God, I believe, granted my husband the special ability to effectively minister to the bereaved.

In addition to burying the dead, the duties of Assignment 4 also included tending to the physical aspects of the church. But we were used to doing the janitorial work, as much as we sometimes deplored the task. In fact, helping my father clean the church had been my dreaded lot as a youngster.

Early one Sunday morning when mute snowbanks hugged the sidewalk between the church and parsonage, Buddy hurried through the cold to turn up the heat in the sanctuary. Inside the auditorium, he felt an unusual warmth. As he stepped over to check the the thermostat, he stopped dead in his tracks. Was he or wasn't he seeing right? Were there actually two feet sticking out over the end of the pew near the head register?

"What goes on here?" he called loudly.

Silence.

The thermostat, Buddy found, had been turned up as far as it would go. This frightened him even more. The furnace could have overheated and set the church on fire. And the nearby parsonage.

Proceeding farther down the aisle, he saw that the conked-out intruder was wearing a bandage on his hand. Turning quickly, he left the building and rushed home. I was still in bed when he returned.

"There's a drunk over in the church," he gasped. "Call the police!"

In a few minutes a policeman pulled up in front, got out of his cruiser, and entered the church. A bit later he reappeared, accompanied by the visitor. When the latter was securely deposited in the police car, the officer came to our door and explained that Kokomo Joe and his wife had had a fight. Kicked out of his house, he began looking for a place to get in out of the frigid weather. When he passed the church, he tried the door. Finding it unlocked, he decided he had found the shelter he was seeking.

But we were to discover that Kokomo Joe had not immediately drifted off to dreamland. There were cigarettes on the piano, an empty pack in the choir loft, and a burned match on the carpeting under the altar. He had left the light on in the ladies' room, and we suspicioned he had been in the office, too.

The Bible says God watches out for fools and little children. Who can dispute it?

Despite my early aversion, in time the too-small parsonage became preferable to moving again. But at first it was not so. As we often do when we are frustrated or cornered, I began looking for alternatives. Perhaps the church would find us another house in which to live. Or maybe they would build.

When all the escape hatches were closed, however, I accepted the situation, arranged the furniture as attractively as possible, and discovered the house wasn't as bad as I had anticipated.

Later on the church board voted to remodel the tiny kitchen. The outdated cupboards and hang-on-the-wall sink were torn out, and lovely birch cabinets were installed. The refrigerator was moved from the corner of the living-dining area to an appropriate spot beside the kitchen range. What a tremendous improvement it all made!

Assignment 4 turned out to be an especially happy and tranquil one. The people received us with warmth and appreciation. They were hospitable, friendly, and loving. Eventually my husband came to accept urban living, although he never learned to like the shifty ground on which we lived.

All in all, those years were exceedingly kind ones, and I remember them with fondness. When we accepted the call to that pastorate, the church was in such a bad financial state that our superintendent could not promise enough money would be forthcoming to meet our weekly salary. But we never missed a paycheck. Furthermore, by the end of the very first year we had met all obligations, installed a new furnace in the parsonage, and painted the exteriors of both buildings.

And God continued to bless us with peace and prosperity. Therefore, when I heard that the church which would eventually become our fifth assignment was looking for a pastor, I was extremely annoyed. (Or was it a premonition?)

"Will you tell your husband the Cumberland church is open?" a preacher friend asked over the phone. "I think he would do well there."

"Yes, I'll tell him," I said, agitated, "but I won't make it sound one bit better than necessary."

"It's a nice church and a good opportunity," the preacher insisted.

"But we don't want to move. We're getting along real well here," I answered pointedly, at the same time pacing nervously between the dining area and the kitchen I now enjoyed so much. "But . . . I'll tell him," I added begrudgingly.

And incidentally, what would we do for a kitchen stove if we moved? I wondered. We had sold our pretty waterfront range when we found that the stove was furnished in this place.

Actually, I was so upset at the thought of moving that I toyed with the idea of not even mentioning the news to Buddy when he came in. Yet, I had promised.

"Honey," I said softly after Buddy returned, "I called Rev. Anson about the meeting Thursday." After some hesitation I added, "He asked me to tell you that the church at Cumberland is open."

"That's funny! Do you remember I said not long ago that I would like to go there some day?"

Yes, I remembered . . . with a grimace!

"But we don't want to move! We like it here! We've just nicely gotten acquainted. The church is making progress, and Sybil is graduating in June. It wouldn't be fair to her if we moved now. And what about her job? She's so happy. I just can't see—"

"Don't worry, Doll, no one has asked for me yet," Buddy interjected, "and they probably won't. I've never told anyone I wanted another church. They would never think of me."

"Can we forget the whole idea then?" I asked hopefully.

"Of course!"

But I could not shake the uneasiness I felt. Each time my husband opened his mouth, I was certain it was to bring up the subject of that church. When he had failed to mention it by nightfall, I began to breathe easier.

8

Assignment 5

The hands on the clock indicated it was exactly 11 P.M. and time to retire. Buddy had checked the thermostat and was heading for the bedroom when the phone rang.

"They've given us a unanimous call to Cumberland?" I overheard him exclaim in surprise. Even before that I had turned numb.

"But we don't want to move," Sybil cried, bounding out of her bedroom across the hall and rushing pell-mell into ours. Following close behind came Sue. She watched in awed silence as her sister flung herself across the foot of our bed and began weeping wildly.

"Honey, if the Lord wants us to move, He will work things out so we're happy," I responded, trying to console her while my whole being cried out against moving, too.

"But Mama, I can't move! You don't know what it's like to move in the middle of the year. I'm graduating!" she sobbed. "Besides, what about my job?"

"O Lord, don't let her be bitter. Please help her," I silently prayed.

Moreover, we did not have to move. There was no obligation involved. My husband had only received an invitation to become pastor of the Cumberland church. He hadn't accepted—yet. He could turn it down.

The next morning Buddy was awake much earlier than usual. "How about taking a trip today?" he asked. "Maybe we ought to go look the situation over before we give an answer. We want to give God a chance to reveal His will to us."

"I think that's a good idea."

"May we go, too?" Both girls stuck their heads around the door. "After all," they said coyly, "it affects us, too."

"OK then. Get your duds on in a hurry."

Hours later, my husband told the outgoing pastor, "This call came as a complete surprise. We are only concerned about doing what the Lord wants us to do. We thought we would come and look things over. Hope you don't mind."

The friendly minister assured us we were entirely welcome. "In fact, I'll be glad to show you around," he said, reaching for his hat, "and maybe the missus will fry us some chicken later on."

But I'll confess I wasn't about to capitulate easily. "What about the high school?" I asked rather bluntly. "Sybil was in hopes of graduating from her Class A school."

"This is a Class A high school," the man replied proudly.

"Oh," I gulped. There went argument number one.

"She has just started working part-time in a dime store. She really hates to give up her job."

"But she can get a job here, I'm sure. They have a new store downtown. It's a real nice place to work."

Sybil perked up—argument number two went flying out the window, also.

"Did you see the college when you came into town?" the minister asked.

"Is there a college in this town?" Buddy asked, astonished.

"A mighty fine one! And it's extremely reasonable."

By attending a local college the next year, our daughter could be with us a while longer. Living at home also meant fewer expenses.

Then I realized that the arguments I had used against moving had been erased, although there were still a couple of problems to be solved. First, we needed a place to live. The church did not own a parsonage. And we soon learned that the house in which the present pastor resided would be put up for sale when they moved out. It would be a real challenge to find a suitable dwelling to rent in that area. Then, too, we needed a stove.

Despite my adamant aversion to moving, I began to search my soul. Yes, I wanted God's will to be done in our lives. If He was leading us to Cumberland, then I must accept it. He would supply our needs and make all of us content.

Nevertheless, it was quite another thing to convince the people in Assignment 4 that we should move.

"These past few days have been like a funeral," I told Ma. "I never saw a church take a pastor's leaving so hard. But I've tried to explain to them that God's will works like a jigsaw puzzle. Everything looks scrambled and mixed up now, but in time the pieces will fit together. The picture will become clear and complete."

So we began making preparations for another move. The previous transitions had been frustrating to me because of the size of the parsonages involved. Now our frustration was due to lack of one. There was a strong possibility that we might have to move into an apartment. That prospect was truly revolting!

The church people at Cumberland kept in touch with us regularly, but each report brought the same message. They could find nothing to rent. Much prayer ascended to the Throne, and in time a phone call brought positive word.

"They've found a house," Buddy said after hanging up the receiver.

"Where?" the girls cried, nearly overpowering him.

"Those people are really rejoicing. They were pretty discouraged. Houses are almost impossible to find."

"How did they locate this one?"

"One of the fellows was driving through town and spotted the tenants moving out. He stopped and inquired about the place and who the owner was. Come to find out, the lady who owns it is a Christian. She had several other bids; but after praying about it, she felt led to rent it to the church."

"Where is it?" the girls insisted. "How far is it from the school?"

"Right across the street; imagine that!"

"Across the street!" they echoed joyously. "Across the street!"

"I heard you say something about carpeting. What was that all about?" I asked. Having a carpeted house was one of my dreams.

"Oh, that! The church voted to buy the carpeting that's down in the house. The renter purchased it just a couple of years ago and decided to sell it to the church instead of moving it."

"Wonderful! Now all we need is a stove."

But we still faced the farewell service in Assignment 4. Saying good-bye to those you've come to love is always difficult for the congregation, pastor, and his family. Although reunions, both on this earth and in the world to come, hold promise, there is still a sadness, a cutting of ties, a finality with which to cope. It can be the most trying aspect of the ministry, especially if the pastor's move comes as a surprise to a congregation reluctant to see him leave, as was the case this time.

I must confess there has been a time or two in our ministry when I could not get away fast enough. Leaving this assignment, nevertheless, was different. I loathed to leave, and the people mourned our going. That made it infinitely harder than ever to be brave. But the promise is ours: "My strength is made perfect in weakness" (2 Cor. 12:9). And His promises never fail.

The last Sunday the people gave us a cash offering for a farewell gift. "We can save this toward a stove," I suggested.

"How much do you think one will cost?"

"We'll have to settle for a used one," I answered emphatically. "That's for sure!"

The following evening, after enjoying heaping dishes of the ice cream Ann and Willie brought with them when they stopped by to bid us farewell, Willie handed Buddy an envelope.

"Five more dollars toward our stove," he announced happily.

Early the next morning before the van arrived, snowflakes began trickling down. By noon a blizzard had set in. The movers had to keep sweeping snow out of the truck while loading the last of the furniture. Finally, they closed the double doors on the rear of the huge van and started out.

We tidied up a bit and walked through the parsonage one last time. I gave a final, lingering look at the birch cupboards over which I had spent so much time and energy planning and supervising their installation. "It's almost like leaving one of the children," I concluded.

By the time our journey was half over, the storm was raging. The wind was blowing madly. Snow fell so fast and furiously it completely obscured sight of the road. Before reaching our destination, travel was practically impossible.

Struggling through the blinding avalanche, we crept forward, moving ever so slowly. At times only the guardrails beside the highway were distinguishable. Frigid wind and snow pelted our faces mercilessly as we searched for glimpses of the highway through opened windows. Straining eyes and nerves, we fought to stay off the yellow line on the left and out of the ditch on the right. After a seemingly interminable time, what a great relief it was to eventually pull up in front of the brightly lighted house which would serve as our temporary home.

In spite of the appalling weather conditions, many of the church people were there to welcome us with a delicious meal and to help with the unloading and settling.

When the van failed to arrive, we began wondering if it would make it. Perhaps it had gone off the road and turned over in a ditch somewhere. Or come head-on with another vehicle.

"While we're waiting, let's go see about a stove," my husband suggested.

"What can you possibly do in this storm?" I asked. "You can scarcely see to drive, much less shop for a range."

But my remonstration fell on deaf ears. I turned from the window with a sigh as Buddy, accompanied by one of the church men, drove away.

After what seemed like an eternity, the van pulled up in front. Soon the movers were unloading our possessions and carting them inside. With each trip came more of the snow that fell unrelentingly.

A bit later Buddy returned, bubbling over with good news. "We found a beauty of a stove for $30.00," he announced. (That, miraculously, was the precise amount given to us before our departure from Assignment 4.)

"You don't mean it!" I exclaimed between my instructions to the movers and those settling the furniture.

"This good man has a pickup out back. We're going after it now."

"An apartment-sized stove?" I asked.

"No, it's a full-sized range—in wonderful condition. Very clean."

Later when everyone had gone, we stood admiring our new acquisition. The burner was glowing brightly.

"It works," Buddy said, as if he half disbelieved what he saw.

"It's a beauty, all right! Why, it looks almost like new."

"We'd have paid 10 times as much if it were."

"Isn't it marvelous how God looks out for His own?" (By the way, we used that stove for several years; and when we finally sold it, we received more than our initial investment.)

In a short time we were nicely settled in the rented "parsonage." The girls were thoroughly and happily adjusted to school. And Sybil had the job she wanted, and was delighted.

Not only had God proved beyond all shadow of a doubt that He was leading and directing our lives (how we would need that assurance later on!), but He was about to do some wonderful things for the church, too. In fact, He had already answered prayer when He gave them a house to rent.

It was a comfortable place to live and the girls especially enjoyed the proximity to the school, but it was distressing to see rental money going down the drain. The cash outlay could be making payments on permanent property—if we could possibly accumulate enough for a down payment, if we could find a place for sale that the church could afford, and if we could find it in the proper location.

Buying a parsonage became a matter of prayer. This relatively new congregation had undergone severe financial stress almost from the beginning. For over a dozen years they had rented housing because they could not accumulate enough for a down payment.

Then, as He had done before when we were in question about buying a house for ourselves years before, God gave me an idea. Why not start with a Parsonage Sunday, using all the money that came in that day toward a down payment? My husband approved and the church board concurred.

The first drive netted us several hundred dollars, and we began looking. Later, a second one increased our nest egg by nearly $500 more. Then, at last, we found a house. A tremendous bargain. But the owners held out for more of a down payment than we could produce.

After some dickering my husband successfully persuaded the owners to reduce their price still further, and a generous member offered to loan the church the balance of the initial payment.

Presto! We had our parsonage—a lovely home on a tree-shaded street. At last, I had elbow room—with some to spare. There was real cause for rejoicing when we moved the second time—again on a November day, but during balmy weather.

In the meantime we had accepted another challenge. It concerned the unfinished church auditorium. The dingy plasterboard faintly resembled a gloomy medieval dungeon. Purple glass had been installed in all the windows with dire consequences. The unlighted room was so dark you could not walk safely down the aisle to the altar at midday when the sun was shining on the outside (I know because I tried it). The floor was bare. The uncomfortable wooden pews closely resembled unpainted park benches. (One young fellow solved his problem, much to our amusement, by bringing a gaily colored cushion to church. It was doubly humorous when he escorted his girlfriend.)

One at a time, slowly but surely, God worked miracles for us, just as He had done many times before. First, a donation provided for the replacement of the windowpanes, enabling the sunlight to enter. Later, the floor was tiled; the platform, carpeted; the interior walls, plastered. Pews were purchased through individual donations. Indirectly lighted crosses were installed behind the pulpit on the inside and on the exterior of the building. At last we welcomed visitors with pride.

In addition to the acquiring of the parsonage and the completion of the church interior, we witnessed many other victories. Wonderful times of blessing were enjoyed around the altar when people sought and found spiritual help. Sinners were converted. Believers were filled with His Spirit when they committed their lives fully to God. Several received a call to special service.

And the devil got mad. Good and mad!

9

Trial by Fire

Old Sam was undoubtedly the greatest miracle to happen during those years. He found the Lord for the very first time after passing the 60 mark. Immediately he set about to salvage what he could of a vastly wasted life. Although he could not undo the harmful influence he had had on his children, he shed many tears of remorse and filled his latter years with prayers for the souls of his lost loved ones.

Sam got drunk on his 13th birthday and stayed drunk much of the time thereafter. Night after night he frequented the village bar.

"Here's Old Sam," his cronies guffawed.

"Here's Old Faithful!"

"How about buying me another one?"

As a lad Sam had watched every move his older brothers made. He also had an uncle, the apple of his eye, who was mean and tough. These evil men were his heroes. When they used God's name in vain, he cursed also. When they drank, he followed suit, sneaking liquor to get drunk.

But tobacco was his worst enemy. There was nothing Sam would not do when he was out of it. That affected him worse than being out of drink.

As Sam's sons grew into manhood, he introduced them to the same vices. He taught them to chew and smoke, take God's name in vain, and drink liquor and other intoxicating beverages. When he wanted them to work on Sundays, he bribed them with draughts of liquor. So many trips around the field behind the plow or cultivator earned them a swig from the ever-present jug.

But God's amazing grace made a vastly different man of Sam. His own nine children were now grown, but a little granddaughter eagerly awaited his return from work to ask for his prayers when she was ill. How different! His children had pretended to be asleep when he came in so he wouldn't hurt them.

The church was uplifted by his testimonies and shouts of praise. Deliverance from the tobacco habit was a special source of blessing to him. "Nothing could have saved me from that awful stuff," he testified, "nothing but the love of Jesus and the power of God."

Despite our times of rejoicing, however, the devil saw to it that we had our share of trials and tribulations. Although I confess that mine were "light afflictions" compared to my husband's, still they were very real.

From the very start I felt I would never get out of that town alive. The impression was so real I talked to our family doctor about it. Time proved that that, too, was a lie of Satan, but it did not lessen the agony.

One does not have to pastor any church for long until one begins to note its imperfections. No assignment is perfect. Nor will it ever be until Satan is bound, gagged, and deprived of his power. After many years in the ministry, we came to look on the first six months of any stay as the "honeymoon." Likewise, we learned to make the most of the pleasant weather before the winter gales set in.

My number one trial had to do with acceptance. As an outgoing, fun-loving person, understanding the shy, taciturn people in the congregation was a real challenge. (And to be fair, I suppose I was a conundrum to them, also.) A lack of approval, however, is an extremely difficult cross to bear.

Now it is both heartening and amusing these many years later to hear, from those clerics who followed us, how much the people loved us. If we'd only realized it then, how different things might have been.

If seeds of fearfulness and suspicion have been sown early in one's life, they are bound to produce fruit of like kind. Furthermore, human feelings of shyness cause some individuals to react hesitatingly toward all leadership. Acting as if the person held in awe does not exist eases their tension, perhaps. If so, their response may not be due to intentional malice. Now I am certain it wasn't.

In the privacy of their homes these people were friendly, generous, and warmhearted. Publicly, some appeared to freeze. Being ignored, even though the snub may be unintentional, is very hard to take, especially if one has a strong need for acceptance. Repeated instances of rejection caused severe emotional pain. Suffering hurt after hurt leads to real mental anguish.

Furthermore, giving out of love and warmth when it is not returned is never easy. But it is something every minister and his wife must do, or they will develop spiritual melanoma.

Fun-loving Beatrice was a lifesaver for me. Having moved to the area when we did, she was lonely and had trouble adjusting, too. I wasn't the only one who longed to feel accepted. Moreover, she possessed a sense of humor that needed ventilating occasionally just as mine did. Neither felt our buffoonery was appreciated by this somber group, however. Attempts to lighten the chilly atmosphere only produced more puzzlement for us both.

One night we experienced the height—or depth—of consternation.

A shower was being given for one of the girls in our group, and Beatrice offered me a ride. Neither of us was looking forward to another starchy, straitlaced evening. On the

74

spur of the moment I picked up the pair of abominably dirty work gloves that were lying on the front seat of her car.

One professional comedian used to declare, "The devil made me do it." Undoubtedly he should be blamed for my action, too. Whatever, I succumbed to temptation, human or otherwise, and slipped my hands into those gruesome grubbies.

"I guess I'll wear these into the house," I said, chuckling, mentally visualizing how ridiculous a sight it would make. Sunday-go-to-meeting dress—and those heinous canvas gloves.

"Why don't you? And watch the expression on their faces!"

By then we were both rollicking with laughter.

Certainly we were not prepared for the reaction we received. Instead of responding as we had expected, the ladies simply ignored the whole scene, acting for all the world as if I had worn those revolting gloves as part of my attire on purpose. How they could ever overlook the hilarity in that masquerade is far beyond me. I must confess that Beatrice and I were dumbfounded. And yes, I was infinitely embarrassed. Nevertheless, the recollection has given us many a good laugh since.

My number two trial centered around the former pastor's wife. The people would not let me forget the meals she cooked, the tremendous chicken she fried, and the washings she took in to help the unfortunate. And I must confess I had a hard time overcoming the temptation to envy and resentment. After becoming personally acquainted with this lovely lady, however, I could understand their appreciation. (But I still wonder if she was aware of their feelings while she lived among them.)

After we left that assignment, the succeeding pastor's wife met with a similar dilemma. She was expected to write for publication as I had done. But her talents did not lie in that field. She was no more able to dash off articles and stories than I had been able to fry chicken to perfection.

Where preachers' wives (or anyone else, for that matter) are concerned, individuality must be accepted and honored. Each pastor's wife must walk in her own shoes. Trying to wear another woman's slippers causes disaster. Endeavoring to be something you're not rubs the heels, pinches the toes, and produces painful emotional corns and calluses.

As I said, my husband had his own tribulation. For a time all went well, except for an unusual number of miscellaneous problems which any pastor faces when serving a church family.

But then, "sudden destruction"! How sad that the events of the final months had to eclipse much of the joy of the earlier years!

From the clerical side of the fence it isn't easy to understand the thinking of laymen who react antagonistically toward those whom God has placed in positions of authority. Perhaps their actions may be due to personal infirmities, not pure and unadulterated evil. If people are dissatisfied with their personal lot in life, it is easy to see why they take out their frustrations on others. If they are looking for a reason to ventilate their inner conflicts, almost any excuse will do.

The first bomb fell very unexpectedly, ripping a vast hole in my husband's sensitive spirit. On a Sunday when he felt especially touched by the presence of the Lord, he openly vented his emotion with praise and tears of joy.

Soon after, one of the church's prominent members made an appointment to see him. "What are you trying to hide?" she asked. "What have you done? What are you covering up?"

Totally shocked that anyone would ever question his moral and spiritual integrity, Buddy was utterly floored. Following on the heels of that incident, several church members grew rapacious and pounced on him with "gnashing teeth."

A visiting minister, one who had contributed liberally to this church, had come to town, and my husband had asked him to speak. Later, Buddy instructed the treasurer to give this man a small token of appreciation for his services. This insignificant expenditure came to light soon after. And it was the spark that ignited the holocaust.

"I move the pastor consult the board before spending any money after this," an indignant member exclaimed, his face turning red.

"Do you mean he must refrain from all spending—not even $10.00 as in this case?"

"Yes! That's what I mean!" the man answered, his vehemence mounting.

"Do you mean the pastor should never ask anyone to fill the pulpit without first consulting this board—even when visitors happen to drop in?" the pastor asked in disbelief.

"Yes! Yes! That's right! Absolutely no spending without permission!"

By now the entire group was aroused.

"I agree," shouted another dissenter, throwing an arm into the air.

"That's right! That's what I say!" heatedly echoed a third.

"No preachers! No preachers!" someone cried out hysterically.

Several more were on their feet now, waving their arms wildly and shouting out their opinions. Bedlam had broken loose. While one man continued his tirade and those who agreed with him ranted like madmen, and some remained silent when they should have been defending their pastor, my husband sat down meekly and watched the rockets flare and listened to the bombs fall.

Although outnumbered and outshouted, two courageous, conscientious gentlemen came to the pastor's defense, but they were no match for the enemy.

Then and there, Buddy realized that the time of his departure was at hand.

A few days later, one dear soul called to apologize for failing to support her pastor that night, but she was the only one. Nevertheless, others, I do believe, have sincerely regretted their indiscretion since then—for several have made a concerted effort to "show" us so. Certainly they should have recognized my husband's wisdom, his efficient management of finances after the judicious purchase of the parsonage and the other accomplishments which had been made. In fact, the church was enjoying the best income in its history. The congregation was prospering. But that only added to Satan's wrath.

Since I want to be entirely fair and charitable, at the next board meeting one of the most vocal dissenters suggested that the pastor be granted the privilege of making insignificant expenditures in the future. His motion carried.

I confess that we were fallible and imperfect. I also wonder if we failed that time. During a former assignment, we took it by the job and prayed down our adversary. This time Buddy decided to move on.

"It would be different if there were only one with whom to cope," he explained.

However, it was distinctly evident that the battle involved several on the opposing team. It simply wasn't worth the "passle to hassle," and he immediately put in his application for a move, something that took months to achieve. And it wasn't easy to wait.

James said that "the trying of your faith worketh patience" (1:3). Even in this excruciatingly hurtful experience, the Lord was working in our lives, helping fit us for the future.

Thank God for the unwavering loyal few who stood by us through thick and thin, who bravely "laid down their own necks" (Rom. 16:4) to offer us their love and support. How pastors and their wives appreciate the courageous minority who remain faithful, willing to sacrifice their own position and favor with their peers, who stand by the called of God when the chips are down and the going is rough. Such friendships are never forgotten and are cherished through the years.

Then, too, there are those who see their mistakes belatedly and seek to rectify them. They are forgiven—even before they ask—or if they never do.

The miracle of this trial by fire was the keeping power of the Holy Spirit. My husband was deeply hurt. He was humiliated and disheartened, but he maintained a sanctified calm though it all. I know because I lived through it with him.

(Nor was that the only time he found God's grace to be sufficient. Once when he was elected to serve on a prestigious board, the name of a pastor of a larger church appeared in his place when the selection was made public. Still Buddy chose to remain silent and sweet-spirited.)

An outsider would never have guessed there had been so much as a suggestion of contention during our stay had he attended our farewell service. As the people passed by shaking hands, crying, embracing, I must confess that I felt much like a corpse receiving the final respects of the mourners.

Miraculously, the Lord resolved all resentments and enabled us to continue loving. Subsequently, this group has also adequately proven that they really did—and still do—love us. And after many years, we learned how our ministry had had a stabilizing effect on that church, how the congregation had benefited financially and spiritually. It does pay to turn the other cheek!

Isn't it wonderful how the difficult places in life can be blessings in disguise if we take a positive attitude toward them? "The trial of [our] faith, being much more precious than of gold that perisheth, though it be tried by fire" (1 Pet. 1:7) can serve to strengthen and prepare us for what lies ahead.

10

Next Move

When I told a former pastor of the church that we had accepted Assignment 6, he replied brusquely, "You'll have to have a strong constitution."

That response certainly added no fuel to the flame of my desire to move to that place, especially after the stress and strain we had been through during the preceding months.

Fortunately, however, his trials were not to be ours. Aside from my initial disappointment at finding bare floors in the parsonage when we arrived, we quickly and happily adjusted to our new surroundings.

Again we moved in November. Friends brought in a hot supper on moving day. Soon after our arrival, another lady rang the front doorbell and handed me a delicious Dutch apple pie when I greeted her. Always such kindnesses are heartening to a pastor and his family who arrive in a new place feeling much like displaced persons.

As I said, one pastor's challenge may not become another's. Two or more individuals react differently in any situation. Furthermore, churches and people constantly change.

But we soon realized we had a specialized work to do in this place as well. The challenge was a bit different from anything we had hitherto experienced, for like siblings, each church in the family of God has a personality all its own. Each calls for personalized understanding and treatment.

"We love everyone!" soon became our battle cry. And gratefully, that love was unanimously returned.

Again, God worked miracles. Before we left that assignment, Fannie said, "The whole church has changed. The people are so different. You folks, both of you, just ooze with love."

That was one of the nicest compliments we have ever received.

*   *   *

My husband was called to the humble home of Grandma Mather and her crippled daughter, Dorothy, to settle their disputes many times. One of these elderly women had threatened to hit the other one over the head with a big club on one occasion.

When the telephone calls came, Buddy drove to their house and talked turkey to these unfortunate souls. Before leaving, he always prayed for them in a personal way. Tears of remorse coursed down their cheeks and promises to behave themselves from now on erupted from their lips. But their good intentions vanished about as quickly as ice cubes in a July sun. After an interlude of compatibility, they were back to their old tricks, and our telephone would ring.

In another assignment it had been the Hosmers brothers. They had feuded for years. When their hostility erupted on the baseball field, it created both excitement and shame for the church team.

Oftentimes undercurrents of animosity exist between families in a congregation for decades. Feelings of resentment, dislike, or jealousy may have begun over incidents which happened long ago. The reason may even be lost to conscious memory, but the resulting antagonism is passed down from generation to generation and erupts periodically. Unrequited love or broken engagements may give birth to lifetimes of contention or cold war. Often conflicts within

81

family groups prove stickier to deal with than those between different family lines.

Keeping an impartial attitude toward all the members of any congregation is far from easy. If one must act as an arbitrator or clerical secretary of state, it is a most demanding chore, requiring more than human expertise and wisdom.

First, there had been Bertha and Beulah to keep on compatible terms. Later in another place it was Tina and Kris.

"Have you called on Kris yet?" Tina kept asking. "You'll really like her. She's so efficient and talented. Did you know she's the president of the local PTA? I sure hope you can get her back in church."

So we went to work on Kris—and we liked her immediately. She was all Tina said she was—charming, talented, an unusual person. She was a leader and very capable. Soon she occupied an active place within the congregation. How happy we were to have her and her lovely family attending the church again!

Then the tide turned. The very person who had begged us to "go after" Kris, changed. Finally, Tina herself left the church.

Oh, consistency! Thou art a jewel!

Arbitrating disputes among church people is, as I said, sticky business. Remaining impartial while loving everyone involved is not easy. Understanding the viewpoints of diverse opinions calls for a degree of specialized talent. Naturally one can see the strengths and weaknesses of both sides. Usually the arguments boil down to six of one, and a half dozen of the other. Yet the peacemaker must listen sympathetically to all and run his comments through a sieve before expressing them.

Added to this, one must continually be on guard lest in a moment of provocation, one lets slip a confidence. There are times when the disclosure of secrets could hasten the resolution of conflicts, but one must stymie utterance. With the parsonage crew it is bottle up or pack up.

Keeping secrets calls for self-abnegation. Being human, it is sometimes extremely difficult not to repeat confidential or interesting inside information. Who doesn't gain at least a smattering of satisfaction by rehearsing a juicy bit of news or a shocking revelation?

The clerical couple hears it all—illegitimate babies, long since forgotten; broken engagements; nervous breakdowns; questionable pasts; annulments; shotgun weddings; divorces; remarriages; unfaithfulness; sexual maladjustments and perversions; scandals; personality hurts; imprisonments; financial failures; unpaid bills; unmade restitutions; infatuations; domestic incompatibilities; dishonesties; personal eccentricities; ad infinitum. All these and more become the inside information of the parsonage. And the inhabitants must develop the ability to forget or trust God for grace and strength to live with closed lips.

Another thing I must confess: It isn't easy to refrain from making close friendships within a church group while serving it as pastor, especially when individuals possessing kindred tastes, talents, and temperaments are involved.

Naturally, it is normal for the parsonage family to like (like, *not* love) some personalities better than others. Frankly, it takes less effort to enjoy being around sweet-smelling, personable guys and dolls than it does to associate with human beings who possess offensive body odors, discordant ideals, and opposite interests.

Although God's love within our hearts enables us to love without respect of persons, still one's humanity calls for fellowship with like kind, those whom Anne of Green Gables said "belonged to the race of Joseph."

Furthermore, the loyal individuals who stand by you through thick and thin when the fire is hot and the waters are high are most likely to become lasting links in your chain of friendships. And always there are those whom you help win to the Lord, or to the church, or bind together in matrimony, or develop a mutual closeness to during times of bereavement or anxiety, who remain especially close to you down through the years.

Parsonage life can be a lonely existence, it is true. But it is better to endure the peace of aloneness than to incur the wrath induced by jealousy.

Pastors and wives are often far removed from their immediate families or longtime friends, the people who genuinely care about them as unique human beings. This only adds to the problem of loneliness. In such cases, one may find it best to make friends with other preachers and wives (perhaps of a different denomination) or laymen outside the periphery of one's church group.

Keeping close friendships outside the realm of the immediate assignment is a habit worth cultivating. Besides it is a boon to the nervous system to be able to let your hair down occasionally. Constantly censoring everything you say—as you must do when conversing with members of your congregation—is nerve-racking business.

Ofttimes intimate friendships between pastor and wife and members of the congregation result in heartaches and regret. Some "best" friends are the first to look for another preacher to replace their present pastor. After becoming acquainted with the humanness and weaknesses of the parsonage clan, some are disillusioned. Or when their curiosity is satisfied, they begin yearning for new fields to conquer. Remember the saying "Familiarity breeds contempt"?

Although a warm welcome is always gratefully received, it often pays to take it easy with those who "wine and dine" you upon your arrival. They may be the first to leave the church disgruntled. It is sad but true that those who "eat you up" on first sight may be the ones who will wish they had ere the honeymoon is over.

Occasionally there are those who seek to buy the control of the pastor and/or his wife. While we appreciate gifts and good treatment, we must never allow ourselves to feel obligated to anyone within a congregation. Nor can gifts buy salvation. They may serve to salve guilty consciences, but they never purchase freedom from sin.

It is true that some of our most cherished friends are former parishioners whose friendships have endured for many years. In some incidences these were the very people who were pleasant and kind to us in the beginning of our stay but a bit slower in making their advances. Always there are exceptions to every rule. I have also noticed that those who spoke kindly about a former pastor upon our arrival were the ones who usually proved to be loyal to us, likewise.

Unfortunately there are a few who seek to "be in good with the preacher" for ego reasons or to have privileged information. Maria worked for the former pastor's wife, so she felt she had earned the right to be on the inside of things. Nellie had once lived in a parsonage, so she, too, believed this earned her intimate footing within the parsonage realm.

How do you let these persons know you love them but you are obligated to treat everyone alike? How do you prevent these poor souls from feeling rebuffed? The only answer I can come up with is this: Show no partiality, but occasionally and sagaciously give these emotionally starved (and perhaps immature) individuals a bit of special attention. No doubt a word of explanation also may be in order.

Certainly the problem of remaining impartial is a challenge to the parsonage clan. The clerical family is as thoroughly human as the lawyer's, baker's, or candlestick maker's. Nevertheless, when it comes to having intimate friendships within a congregation, cautious treading is called for.

It is my personal opinion, however, that the restrictions placed on the preacher and his wife need not be applied to their offspring. Why should children be penalized because of their father's profession? This conviction brought me one of my severest trials.

During an earlier assignment, I came home from church one Sunday morning to find both our girls in tears. Sympathizing with them were their brokenhearted "best friends."

"What in the world has happened?" I asked, looking aghast from one tear-stained face to another. "What is wrong?"

"Mrs. Baker says we can't be friends anymore," Sybil sobbed.

"She said what?"

"She said preachers' children shouldn't have special friends."

Struggling to maintain my composure, I assured the four pathetic little creatures that they could go on being friends, comforted them the best I could, and suppressed my indignation.

Mrs. Baker of all people! It was a well-known fact that she and her husband hobnobbed intimately with another couple in the church. Sometimes they were together until the wee hours of the morning. And she had the audacity to mercilessly jump on our children, utterly crushing them with her unreasonable demand!

Contrary to my placid nature, that time I had all I could do to restrain myself. Maybe I should have followed my impulse and set her straight.

But I didn't. The children's feelings healed. And so did mine—eventually.

*   *   *

But I must confess we have been truly blessed. Despite a few disappointments, God has privileged us to live and work among some of the best people on earth. And to many we owe a special debt of gratitude.

Every pastor and wife should deeply appreciate those individuals who volunteer their baby-sitting services. For us, among others, there were the Babbs, an elderly southern couple, who took our girls in and gave them the best of care when we were out of town.

Next came Grandma Amburgey, who fed them the sugar cookies they liked so much. Following that, a succession of other kindhearted souls opened their hearts, homes, and pocketbooks to our children. A few single women moved in with them temporarily when we were away. To all these dear ones who gave so generously to our family, we are eternally indebted.

Those persons who cheerfully and lovingly look after the parsonage young naturally come under the category of "special people."

11

Tragedy and Triumph

Assignment 6 brought us one of the most demanding tasks we would face in our ministry. During Assignment 2, tragedy had struck when one of our Sunday School boys was killed instantly by a stray bullet while playing in the creek behind his home. It was our first experience dealing with parents suddenly bereft of a child. Then it was one parent, a widow, who lost her younger son. To go to her in her hour of shock and grief had seemed an utterly impossible thing to do for me, but God's strength proved sufficient, as it invariably does whatever the demand may be that is placed on us.

Now it was years later. Cold rain pelted the windows, and a sharp autumn wind whined plaintively. Answering a knock on the front door, I recognized our family doctor.

"Is your husband here?" he asked excitedly.

"He's at the church. You'll find him there," I told him. "Has something happened?"

"Freddy Benson was just killed. He was riding his bicycle on the highway," he replied hurriedly.

Minutes passed. Buddy returned to the parsonage and said, "The doctor asked me to go out and tell the Bensons that Freddy has been hit by a car."

"Oh no!"

"We'll have to go."

"I can't!"

"Yes, you can! The Lord will help us. Brace up. It's part of the ministry."

"Is the doctor going with us?"

"No, he thinks a minister should do it."

By the time we reached the scene of the accident, for we had to pass it to get to the Benson home, a crowd had gathered on the highway.

"You can't get through," the policeman said, stopping us.

"I'm Rev. Spray," my husband explained.

Immediately a path was cleared. Praying desperately for strength and guidance, we proceeded. A bit later we stepped inside the Benson home and stood waiting in the doorway.

"I've come to tell you there's been an accident . . ."

"Something's happened . . . someone's been hurt . . ." the mother gasped.

Silence.

"Someone's been killed?"

We could only look our assent.

"It can't be!"

We waited.

"Are you sure? When did it happen?"

At that point the father, a gruff-appearing man, entered from another doorway. "What's wrong?" he demanded.

"There's been an accident," my husband replied.

"George! George! Where's George? George!" the woman called hysterically.

"It's not George," Buddy said.

"Not Freddy! No! Not Freddy!"

Silence.

"It's those bikes! I told him! I told him!" the distraught woman screamed.

"I told him!" wailed the father, quickly exiting the room by the same door he had entered, leaving us frightened and perplexed. Was he angry at us for bringing the news?

"Freddy Dale. Freddy Dale," Mrs. Benson whispered in a state of shock and disbelief. "O God Almighty, not another one!" she moaned. "Why did God give them to us if He was going to take them away?"

Then the father was back. "It can't be! It isn't true!" he exclaimed, pacing the floor and crying like a baby.

"Oh no! No! No!" The mother was now screaming and smashing at the wall with her fists. She pushed her wet face into a corner and continued screaming until she fell in a heap on the floor.

An older girl rushed into the house and fell on her mother. Two smaller children watched in wide-eyed silence. An older brother entered in a state of shock. He too began to cry.

Very quietly my husband began to pray. Almost immediately the whole family grew calm.

At last the mother, spent with emotion, raised up. "You kids get upstairs," she shouted at the smaller ones. What kind of thoughts must have raced through their little heads! Why didn't I go to them? I have wondered since. But frankly, I didn't quite know what to do myself, and I was occupied with trying to help the mother.

Telephone calls had to be made and funeral arrangements cared for. Although the children attended our Sunday School, the parents were Catholic, so a priest was engaged to hold the funeral service. However, my husband, a Protestant minister, and I sat with the family during the requiem mass. It was the first, and so far the last, time we have been asked to do that. Perhaps this was what the apostle Paul meant in part when he wrote, "I am made all things to all men, that I might by all means save some" (1 Cor. 9:22).

*   *   *

90

On a happier note, God granted us another miracle of conversion when Les, like Old Sam, also in his 60s, found the Lord for the first time during our stay in Assignment 6.

Early one Monday morning the telephone rang. "Les wanted me to call and see if you are going to be home this evening," Alva said.

All day we wondered why he wanted to see us. True, I had known Alva since childhood, but we had lost track of each other following the breakup of her first marriage. Then one Sunday, out of the blue, she and her present husband, Les, attended the morning worship service. What a surprise to learn they lived not far away! Soon they were coming to church regularly. The day before, they had brought relatives, too.

Life had not been easy for either of them. A few years earlier, after divorces, they were brought together by a mutual acquaintance. Alva could not get away from her earlier teachings despite the many years she had strayed from the Lord. Then she began to pray and read the Bible. "He sure has helped me," she said. "I know I have Him in my heart."

On Sunday my husband had preached a pungent message on faith, little realizing the profound effect it was having on Les.

At 6:30 that Monday evening we heard a car door slam. After taking their coats and his hat and chatting a bit, Les told us, "I asked Alva to call and make an appointment because I wanted to come out and see you. I got saved last night."

"Well, bless your heart!" Buddy responded. A moment later he and Les were embracing. And so were Alva and I.

"I've had a glorious day. I don't think I slept a wink last night. I cried all night long," Les continued.

"You're a miracle!" we exclaimed.

"I really don't know how it all happened. I was in bed. Alva was listening to the newscast. When she came in, I told her, 'Something's happened to me. I want to be a Christian.'"

"'Well, let's pray,' I said," his wife continued. "I said, 'Get out of bed and we'll do the best we can. I don't know much about it, but I can try.'"

What a thrill it was to look from one face to the other and note the happiness shining on their countenances.

"He did a pretty good job," Alva went on. "He did all right. He asked the Lord for forgiveness."

"I wanted to come out and tell you because your sermons have brought me to this place," Les explained. "And I wanted you and Pauline to pray for me."

Immediately the four of us were on our knees, rejoicing over the lost sheep that had been found and asking the Lord to strengthen these babes in Christ.

Les was not the only miracle of grace during our stay. Others were also rescued from modern-day heathendom. Young people grew spiritually, and a few began making plans to prepare for special service in the Kingdom.

With the Lord's help we were able to break all previous Sunday School records. Despite some traumatic incidents which required a power beyond our own with which to cope, those years in that assignment were productive ones. And my husband's resignation came as a severe shock to the congregation. Sometimes I wonder if all the people have truly forgiven us for leaving even yet.

12

Assignment 7

The long-distance calls began coming before we scarcely were settled in Assignment 7. One thing is certain: We had no inkling whatsoever as to what we were getting into when we accepted the call to serve this congregation.

The church building, located in a naturally beautiful area, was a lovely new edifice. In addition, the move afforded us a raise in salary—something especially enticing after having lived with heavy expenses for quite some time.

If for nothing more than the human need for success, we all appreciate advancement. A promotion now and then raises the ego and increases one's self-esteem. And we thought Buddy was getting that—a promotion. However, if we had been aware of the financial state of this assignment, he probably would have gladly opted for less.

But, as always, we earnestly prayed about making this move, and we sincerely believed we were in the center of God's will in accepting it. And God proved His faithfulness.

Certainly my husband's predecessor performed a noteworthy feat in getting the church group out of inadequate housing and into attractive facilities. But he left shortly after the victory march from the old to the new building, and before the bills were paid. My husband, therefore, inherited the colossal task of clearing the name of the church with its creditors and making it financially solvent again. That involved many tensions.

Our initial response to the long-distance requests for money was shock. After some persistent probing of the reticent treasurer, Buddy discovered to his intense dismay that the congregation was overloaded with debts. It was saddled with heavy denominational obligations, massive local bills, a ponderous church payment, and a parsonage payment. He also learned, much to his chagrin and consternation, there were two additional bank loans, amounting to many thousands of dollars, to be repaid in installments. The accumulated monthly obligations were far more than we could handle on our modest income. This put the new building in jeopardy. For months it looked like the people would lose their duly prized edifice. (Incidentally, another group was making plans to move in when we threw in the sponge, so we heard via the grapevine.)

But prayer prevailed.

Miraculously, little by little, the smaller bills were paid; the loans were whittled down; the monthly payments were somehow met, if only by the skin of our teeth. And these were indeed miracles! Each and every one.

Then came another shock! We received word that a court order would be obtained to close the church doors unless the congregation carried through with an earlier promise to construct a high wooden fence along two sides of the property, a project involving many hundreds of dollars—which the church did not have. The treasury was already overloaded and could not possibly bear up under another smidgen of strain.

Then through the generosity of the one who paid for the lumber and the donated labor of several other men, the fence was built. And the church doors remained open. Another miracle.

Following that, we were greeted with still another shocker. A telephone call from the asphalt company informed us the church owed them many hundreds of dollars, also. This included the initial debt, plus the accrued interest over a long period of time.

My husband was absolutely floored. Would the revelations never cease? In spite of his efforts to ascertain the true financial status of the congregation, the jolts kept coming.

This time he made a personal visit to the business establishment to beg leniency. Through an additional miracle, the company agreed to drop the accumulated interest if the principal were paid immediately. Therefore, another spurt of concerted effort enabled the church to come through, and with God's help the debt was liquidated.

Besides all this, there was yet another financial challenge with which to cope. Whoever drew up the architectural plans for the church building, involving a gigantic window which extended from floor to cathedral ceiling, did not reckon with the location of the setting sun. On summer evenings the blinding western rays were disastrous.

The pastor was badgered by complaints. Pressure was increasingly applied to purchase a covering for the aperture. Already under undue tension by the many financial demands, he felt he could take on no more. Finally in desperation he told an insistent parishioner, "If you want a curtain, you will have to raise the money yourself."

That instigated still another drive. Thousands of dollars were raised through individual gifts to purchase and install an immense velvet drapery to care for the incapacitating sunsets.

And peace again reigned.

Shortly before we moved, the financial state of the church was under control. All the superfluous bills were paid. Only the regular payments and expenses remained, and these the church was at last able to handle. I must confess we could not have done it without the Lord's help and the sacrificial cooperation of the people. In addition, our church leaders charitably granted this congregation a period of grace where denominational obligations were concerned during this time.

The task was not easy. It is difficult to convince some people that while it is easy to make debts, there is also a reckoning day to face. Nor is it an enjoyable task to play disciplinarian. The popularity polls often reflect the consequences. Nonetheless, when one is looking out for God's cause, right must prevail, regardless of the ratings.

We also learned that the one who does the paying may not receive as much earthly applause as the one who does the spending. However, to each his own gift. Both builders and bill-footers are needed in His kingdom. The Lord will make the final tabulations and hand out the eternal rewards.

*   *   *

Years earlier Buddy was chatting amiably with two of our church boys.

"I'd like to be a preacher," one confided, "but the trouble is you have to be ever so smart!"

"Oh no, you don't!" countered the other. "Rev. Spray, here, is!" And the three laughed heartily.

Many men who once called my husband their pastor are presently serving in the ministry, pastoral or otherwise. The reason for this serendipity remains a mystery to Buddy. While I credit it to his understanding and encouragement, he says facetiously, "I guess they think if I can do such a poor job of it and get by, they can preach, also."

Regardless, it is a joy for any minister to witness the reproductive process, to see other men following in his footsteps. To date, one of Buddy's ministerial offspring has shepherded two churches he once pastored.

Perhaps the secret of Buddy's success in reproducing like kind was best revealed by an ordained minister who began attending our services during Assignment 5. He eventually gave up his credentials in another denomination to join our congregation as a lay member.

"Brother Spray didn't *get* me into the church," he explained. "He loved me into it." This man was reordained and became an instructor in one of our largest colleges.

While we strolled on the campground during a church meeting, we watched with amusement as a little boy repeatedly passed us on his bicycle. He was, in fact, the facsimile of an intelligent, snappy, dark-eyed youngster who once attended one of our Sunday Schools.

"Is John S—— your daddy?" we finally asked.

"Yes," the cherubic youngster replied. After some hesitation, he countered, "Are you the man who used to be my father's pastor?"

"Yes . . . when he was a little boy just like you."

"Well, he told me how he liked you so much," the youngster ventured bashfully.

Certainly we never dreamed when we were sharing the hospitality of that lad's grandfather's home that the "original copy" with his bright eyes and eager ears would grow up to become a successful pastor in his own right.

Not all of the men answered their call to preach during my husband's interim as their pastor, but anyone who felt God's thumb in his back was the recipient of his support and encouragement. Each was given the opportunity to try his wings in the pulpit if he was sincere and willing to test his flying ability.

Because of their ages, family obligations, and lack of education, some men felt doomed to live with a sense of unfulfillment. When they confessed their predicament, Buddy inspired them to follow the call of God by seeking to prepare —even at a late date in their lives. Not long ago Beecher and Evelyn, in their late 50s, left behind 10 grown children and umpteen grandchildren to enter Bible college in a distant state. Now they, too, are pastoring.

Despite seemingly impossible barriers, more than one man surmounted the hurdles and is serving in the ministry today.

The telephone messages and letters we receive are indeed gratifying. Sometimes the person upon whom we felt we were making little indentation has surprised us. This goes for Mike who wrote: "We . . . wanted to . . . tell you how much we have appreciated you both. I am sincere when I say that of all the preachers I have heard, none has had as great effect on my life as has your ministry. . . . I can still recall clearly many of the sermons you preached."

Wendall, in his mid-20s, was bright, personable, and gifted, but his spiritual life continually seesawed. He was a concern to those who loved him, especially his equally talented, charming wife.

One night while I was counseling her, she sobbed, "It's Wendall."

"Jean, are you willing to forgive him for anything he may have done—no matter what?" I asked, aware of the immense challenge she might be facing.

"Yes, anything," she wept.

"Then go home and tell him just that."

Wendall soon came to the place where he was determined to give God complete control of his life and to live in total obedience. He began to make restitutions for wrongs of long standing and did not stop until he had righted his past and washed his slate clean. He became an entirely different man. So different, everyone who knew him noted the miraculous change in his life.

While lunching with Wendall and Jean, they told us they had decided to return to college and prepare for Christian service. Later he wrote: "I would, first of all, like to thank you and Mrs. Spray for . . . the help you have given us knowingly, and the help you have been unknowingly. We were a little skeptical in the beginning, but as time went by we could see the . . . strength you and your wife had. This has been a tremendous help to us, seeing that no matter what opposition or difficulties arise it can be taken in stride and overcome with God's help."

Wendall finished school, and for several years he and his wife have been making a valuable contribution to the work of the Lord.

The night before we moved to a certain assignment years before, a young woman left her husband and children. Many times during our stay, little Billy went to the altar to sob like his heart would break in two while praying for his mother's return.

Now a married man, a graduate of seminary, he recently took his first pastorate. We were delighted to hear from him not long ago. Among other things, he said, "I wish to thank you both for the ministering and sharing you gave to my dad and us kids . . . The song you sang as a duet, 'I'm a Millionaire,' has come back to me many times . . . You seemed so happy . . . Thank you for your living witness and inspiration to my young life."

Lillie was another miracle. I met her in our neighborhood grocery store. When I asked her to cash a check from our publishing company, she told me she and her husband met and were married in a church of our persuasion in another city.

Naturally I invited her to attend our services.

Some time later, on a very stormy night, our telephone rang.

"I've got to talk to someone," a feminine voice insisted. "I don't know if you remember me or not."

"Yes, I remember." This raven-haired, blue-eyed, fair-complexioned beauty did not know the number of times I purposely had gone through her checkout lane just to keep in touch with her.

Because many inches of new snow had fallen, our drive was next to impassable. We doubted if she could make it in. But shortly the doorbell rang and I hastened to answer it.

After stepping out of her boots and removing her jacket she began pouring out her story. She and her husband were living far from God and had separated. When their relationship became unbearable and he refused to go, she moved out, leaving six small children behind.

She became a cashier in the store I frequented, but her severe mental state forced her to quit her job. Fearing insanity, she consulted a psychiatrist, who, much to her disillusionment and consternation, propositioned her in his office.

"Where do I go now?" she cried in desperation. "What is there left?"

But God was working—answering not only my prayers but those of loved ones as well.

Lillie and her husband had married during their teens— he out of rebellion toward his parents and the church; and she, out of rebellion and the need for security. In 11 years they had seven children. When their last baby died, Lillie felt that God allowed the tragedy for a purpose.

"I've tried everything," she confessed, "drugs, alcohol, everything. Is there such a thing as getting to the place where God has left you, where you have crossed the deadline?"

My husband assured her that the fact that she was sitting in our family room with tears streaming down her face was proof that God was still speaking to her. Then he suggested we pray.

As the three of us knelt down to pray, this poor, penitent sinner began sobbing her way through to God.

Finally she grew quiet. Very quiet. Then, like a soft summer rain on a hot, dusty day, God's presence came and washed away her guilt, literally bathing her with peace.

I watched with profound fascination as the expression on her face gradually altered. It was as if someone had taken a wet cloth and washed away all the guilt, shame, and despair. The transformation was incredible. But, oh, so wonderful! Only a genuine miracle of the Almighty Heavenly Father could effect such a metamorphosis!

And I must confess, I feel highly honored to have had a small part in helping bring it about.

13

Wear, Tear, and Wedding Bells

The stresses of Assignment 7 took a substantial toll of my husband's strength. Because of my concern for his welfare and happiness, I promised God I would be content wherever He saw fit to send us, if only Buddy were satisfied.

After our move to Assignment 8 I conscientiously kept my word—until an authoritative figure suggested we were misfits. Despite the doubts that statement generated, I honestly tried to keep my promise and make the best of our lot. But I must confess it wasn't easy much of the time. We had been settled in the newly redecorated parsonage (a gesture I deeply appreciated) only a few weeks when trouble set in. However, before I go into that, let me tell you about the weddings.

*   *   *

During Assignment 4 it was funerals. Now, several years and churches later, Buddy was kept busy marrying instead of burying. This assignment beat any when it came to matrimonial knot-tying.

Here couples frequently began attending the church services shortly before their wedding date. That made them eligible to use the attractive sanctuary for their nuptials without charge. Despite the fact that these people often ceased attending church immediately following the ceremony, my husband assented when he could, hoping for an opportunity to minister to the spiritual needs of the families involved. Besides, as he said, "Someone needed to marry them." The promise of a less-than-best marriage beat living in sin, or a ceremony performed by a justice of the peace. Therefore, few couples were turned away, excepting, of course, those marriages my husband was forbidden by the church rules to perform.

To me one of the most rewarding features of being a minister's wife has been the privilege of sharing this intimate, happy time with the wedding couple, their families, and friends. It is the icing on the cake as far as I am concerned. Being asked to assist with the planning, offer suggestions, share ideas, and then, in whatever way possible, help make weddings run smoothly at the last minute is something I have truly enjoyed. At the back of the sanctuary I have given support and quietly prompted ushers, bridesmaids, parents, and the bride, too. My efforts have been rewarded with generous words of appreciation. Having someone to lean on when heads are spinning and the world is topsy-turvy is a boon many never forget.

"What would I ever do without you?" Frances said when Jean got married. That expression of her gratitude was well worth the small contribution in time it cost me.

Since that long-ago day when the photographer mistook him to be a member of the bridal party, Buddy has performed a great variety of weddings—from extremely simple to expensively elaborate occasions, from highly solemn ceremonies to ridiculously humorous and unusual affairs.

The greatest shock came when one couple asked to be married with their feet on the ground—literally. For my sensitive funny bone, this was almost too much. The sight of that bride coming down the aisle in a once-upon-a-time white gown and veil, sans shoes and hosiery, was a mirth-provoking spectacle. Nevertheless, since both bride and groom appeared to be sincere, the bare facts of the matter remained: We hoped their marriage was based on solid footing, got off the ground warmly, and was shod with peace and happiness thereafter.

The wedding of Chris and Cindy is one Buddy certainly remembers and will never forget. Their marriage definitely was a no-nonsense affair. No one could say it was entered into lightly.

The couple was married in the beautiful church auditorium during Assignment 7 in a simple ceremony which turned out to be very short and sweet.

The bride was attractive in the dress which had been made by her grandmother and worn by Cindy's mother on her wedding day.

As for the groom, he was deadly serious about the step he was taking, so serious that the pastor glanced up from his manual to see him, ashen and shaking, about to pass completely out of the picture.

My husband calmly maneuvered the fainting groom to a front seat, sat down beside him, and talked soothingly to him while the bride, attendants, and guests waited in silence.

Standing in the foyer where I had helped direct the bridal party, I wondered if the groom was backing out of making his commitment. This had never happened to us before.

"Do you want to go on with the ceremony now?" the pastor asked after what one could rightly call a "protracted meeting."

Wobbly but willingly Chris stepped forward. He and his charming bride were united in lawful wedlock by means of a ritual shorn of all superfluity.

"This is for good!" my husband overheard the groom whisper to his bride following the exchanging of their vows.

Small wonder.

One of the weddings I thoroughly enjoyed took place during an earlier assignment when Dick came home on furlough from the air force. With little time (or money) to plan or prepare for a wedding, our united efforts produced a memorable occasion. The bride's sister quickly made her gown and veil, and Dick fashioned a candelabra from pieces of wood.

I cherish the picture of that wedding, and I know Phyllis must especially prize hers, for Dick passed away at a very young age, leaving her to raise their children single-handedly.

Another wedding made an indelible imprint on my memory—for a far different reason.

Practically everyone involved in this wedding, except for the bride and groom whom we knew slightly, were strangers to us.

Jesus is no respecter of persons, and my husband tried to follow His example. Regardless of their backgrounds, whether or not they come from the community's upper echelon, each couple was married in a proper and dignified manner.

The guests, obviously friends of the bride's family, were a colorful group—without a doubt the clientele of the queasiest, tackiest bar in the area, but they had made an honest effort to dress for the occasion. However, I wonder if some had ever frequented a church before in their entire lives. Certainly we had not encountered them before—or since.

Nevertheless, it was the bride's mother who stole the show! Surprisingly, most of the wedding—the dresses and flowers—exhibited good taste, but the scrubby brogans the mother wore were an absolute anathema to her attractive, new gown. That seemed to concern her little, if at all. Smugly, serenely, and oozing with satisfaction, she appeared to be as much at home as if she were the piano, organ, or one of the pews. She strutted around with an exaggerated air of importance, acting like she owned the place or paid her tithes regularly, and gleefully watching the faces of her guests for indications of their admiration and approval.

"Ain't this somethun?" you could almost hear her thinking. "Come on, you bums, just look at us! Some class, eh? Makes your eyes bug, don't it?"

Time has yet to erase from my memory the recollection of that proud pseudosocialite and her triumphant masquerade. And I doubt if I ever forget it.

There is another pathetic, but humorous, time I also remember. This time the couple was obligated to pay for the use of the church since they were total strangers who came to us for counsel and assistance.

There was rivalry between the parents of the bride and groom. Since the groom was deaf, his father insisted on serving as his best man. Not to be outdone, the very pregnant mother of the bride, in a much too tight gown, was matron of honor.

Another unusual experience took place on a cold winter night when we drove over slippery, snow-drifted roads to get to a farmhouse far out in the country.

A few days before, we had received a call from an upset mother. The church had been reserved for the wedding of her daughter, but now the girl was violently ill, so ill she could not go through with a public ceremony.

"Would Brother Spray come out here and marry them?"

Who needed to be married more than a pregnant bride-to-be?

When we arrived, the yard was rapidly filling up with cars. Inside, we found the house prettily adorned with Christmas tree lights and other beautiful decorations.

Because of the bride's condition, a sofa was arranged in the living room where the bridal party could be seated. (As an added precaution, a single bed was placed directly behind the sofa in case the bride needed to lie down hurriedly.) On huge red hearts, placed at either end of the couch, appeared the names of the couple in glittering silver letters. Behind these stood the candelabras, adorned with wreaths of white flowers.

In another room, out of sight, someone chopped out the strains of "Here Comes the Bride" on an out-of-tune piano.

Following the entrance of the men, the feeble, wan bride, in a traditional gown and veil, entered on the arm of her youthful-appearing father.

"Who gives this bride away?"

"Her mother and I."

Thereupon the bride, groom, and attendants sat down on the couch and remained seated throughout the ceremony because the woman being married was too weak to stand.

Careful planning, the purchase of beautiful gowns, and much work had gone into the preparations for this wedding. How lovely it would have been in the church auditorium! These people, in spite of the uncommon aspects, deserved a lot of credit for making the best of a disappointing, awkward situation.

A poignant touch followed the tension-packed ceremony. Four or five of the bride's younger brothers and sisters sat on straight chairs lining the bridal path. Following the rituals, the smallest of the lot melted into tears. My eyes, too, misted over at the sight of that perplexed little one.

While most weddings are joyful affairs, they can also be touched by sadness. This was very true of the wedding of Jerry and Pam. Both bride and groom had been in my Sunday School class, and I had grown very fond of them. Several years later, after we had moved a couple of times, they came to visit us and asked my husband to return to their town and perform their ceremony. Shortly after that, it was discovered that Jerry's mother was terminally ill with cancer.

I wondered that June afternoon as I sat in the flower-bedecked, music-filled room if she would be able, or courageous enough, to attend. When her husband and daughters entered, I couldn't help wondering, Will it be like this in just a few more weeks? Will they be without her then?

The hands of the clock pointed to the hour. Soon the ceremony would begin. Then, slowly and regally, with head held high, Kris entered the cool, fragrant room and was coming down the aisle on the arm of an usher.

Wearing a familiar navy dress, a becoming white hat, and a pretty corsage, she was the picture of poise and dignity. Although thin and pale, she was gay and cheerful. This was her son's gala day, and it would be unmarred by sadness.

At the reception she and I visited. Knowing how she had triumphed over many odds in life, I was both fond of her and inspired by her example. There was an especially close bond between us.

"I like your hat, Kris," I told her. "It is very becoming."

"I didn't know if I should buy it or not," she confided. "It really was an extravagance, a waste of money."

No further words were necessary. I knew what she was thinking.

A few months later, Kris was laid to rest in the same dress she had worn to Jerry's wedding. Another corsage was pinned to her shoulder, so terribly thin and cold now. But the white hat was missing. I have often wondered what became of it.

Yes, weddings have come in many shapes and sizes. The two I remember best, however, are the ones we gave our own daughters—on a pittance and plenty of hard work. But I enjoyed every minute of the planning, penny-pinching, conniving, sewing, manipulating, cooking, errand-running, and bargain hunting.

Nor have I forgotten the generosity and helpfulness of the people in the congregations where we were serving at the times of these weddings. Nor the friends from former assignments who traveled many miles to attend the ceremonies and bring their gifts.

The first of these weddings was held in a church with a lighted cross gleaming behind the pulpit. It added such an impressive touch that I longed to have it used for the second wedding, excepting that by this time we were far away.

Obligingly, kind friends took down that cross, transported it all those miles, hooked it up in a different church, took it down when the ceremony was over, and returned it to its original location—all to satisfy the whim of this sentimental mother.

That lighted cross brought continuity to our family experiences, as the Cross does to all of life.

14

Assignment 8

Now as I look back on it, I am amazed that I came through the Assignment 8 years in as good a shape (?) as I did, for it was trouble from start to finish. Of course, there were good times. Times of victory. Even miracles. But in no equal period have I endured more trial and tribulation and experienced such tension. And it all took place during those years, regarded by many as crucial in a woman's life. Only the grace of God kept me sane, saved, and sanctified.

We had been ensconced in the parsonage but a few weeks when the former pastor's wife, and our personal friend, stopped for a brief chat and to see the newly redecorated kitchen. Her hesitancy to leave that day has since caused me to wonder if she instinctively knew it would be her last visit.

Not long after, her husband sadly told us the doctors had found more cancer. Her disease, discovered earlier and temporarily arrested, had erupted again. This time there would be no remission. In six months' time, on a raging winter day, we laid her to rest in a snowy cemetery to await the resurrection morning.

For months, all of us—church people and parsonage dwellers—suffered with Patricia and her family. A beautifully loving person, her uncomplaining acceptance cast an influence on others which left a deep impression.

Her death was not only a personal loss, but I confess the vibes of the grieving congregation also affected me adversely. Did I sense resentment because she died and I lived? She left small children. Mine were grown. Besides, I was a newcomer. An outsider. An intruder. She was one of them. They had shared her shock and grief when her illness was first discovered. They, too, had shared the expectancy and joy a new parsonage baby brought. The bond between them was unusually strong.

But as a partner of the parsonage team, one must teach by example that in times like these one can find consolation in Christ. A yieldedness to His will and unwavering faith bring acceptance.

My husband, also, was faced with a strange and puissant trial. From the very first he recognized it—it was one he had never experienced before.

During his youth Buddy greatly admired fire and brimstone preachers. So he started out copying their style. Although He needs and uses all kinds of messengers, God began to show my husband early in his ministry that his method of sermonizing was to be different from what he had envisioned.

For many years this congregation had sat under strong evangelism. Therefore, Buddy received the task of giving the people what they needed but some did not necessarily want. They were used to hearing the verities of hell and the Judgment frequently expounded. Buddy heralded the virtues of love, faith, and hope. Naturally the drastic change in pulpiteering style was baffling to some. While a few expressed appreciation for his messages, others apparently found them insipid, for after the honeymoon was over, they began seeking more interesting offerings—elsewhere.

Several of the ladies were introduced to a minister who emphasized one of the spiritual gifts. These conscientious souls were captivated by the appeal of his teachings. Eventually they made it known, one by one, that "God told them" to transfer from our fold to what they believed to be a greener and more succulent pasture.

The action of these people was most confusing and distressing to us. These were good Christians and valuable workers. They fasted, prayed, attended faithfully, and contributed unselfishly to the work of the Kingdom.

We never for a minute doubted their integrity or sincerity. And we respected their desire for a closer walk with God. But we wanted that, too. This was the focus of Buddy's messages. Nevertheless, the genuine isn't recognized, oftentimes, unless it comes cloaked in the unusual. A child inevitably chooses a large, bright toy rather than a small, practical gift. Many adults respond likewise to matters of the Spirit.

Another thing we believed, and still do, that God does speak to His people in sundry ways. Hadn't He, years before, spoken to me about buying that little house in the college town in a distinctively urgent way? Hadn't He implanted the idea in my mind about securing a parsonage in another assignment? Hadn't He laid His hand on my life and called me to special service when I was still a child?

Nevertheless, we also know, according to the Scriptures, that all of God's leadings are founded on sound judgments. Furthermore, we are cautioned to "try the spirits" (1 John 4:1). Are they truly of God, of Satan, or are they merely persistent human urges and desires? If we seek after a whim or fancy long enough, God sometimes lets us have it, whether or not it is in our best interest.

To date, this was our most confusing experience in the pastoral ministry. So many "God saids" and "God told me's" came at us, it was excruciatingly perplexing. Also, it was disconcerting to see other people becoming unstabilized and bewildered. I prayed while walking the floor, making beds, doing dishes, hour after hour.

Before the great trek was over, our attendance had dwindled drastically. Eventually, according to their testimony, "God told" our assistant pastor, organist, several Sunday School teachers, with their families, to travel on, and we had the onerous task of answering the questions and stilling the qualms of those who remained behind.

The wounds from these lacerations were still raw when more of our number began to lose interest. Soon they, too, pulled up stakes and journeyed to more enticing feeding grounds.

The departure of so many people who were loved and needed left an aching void in the church family. It meant loneliness, strained relationships, and loss of financial support.

Still God's work must go on. And thank God for the faithful who stuck by the guns in the thick of the battle.

Because of these agonizing wounds, it is comparatively easy to understand why some should turn the blame on the pastor and his wife. But what were we to do but remain unmovable and firm in the faith? After all, the Lord had clearly assured us before accepting this assignment that we were in His will to come. We determined with His help to remain undaunted, refusing to be defeated. And we also determined to love, whether or not it was returned.

Then, as if all this wasn't enough to test one's mettle, Satan struck in another way, making a direct hit on the parsonage. Like he attacked Job, he afflicted my husband with a variety of illnesses. First, Buddy's future in the ministry was threatened when he developed a granuloma on his vocal cords, necessitating surgery. For weeks I was his voice, making calls, overseeing the services, and transmitting two-way messages.

Nor was that the end. In a few more months he suffered a physical breakdown which required more surgeries and months of recuperation from both the surgeries and a heart

113

condition. During this time, except for brief intervals, he continued to care for the church. More than once I watched apprehensively as he preached while holding on to the pulpit to keep from falling.

For me this meant carrying not only my household and writing loads but helping shoulder his responsibilities, too. It also caused me to give up a fully paid trip to the Holy Land, a severe disappointment. Furthermore, I must confess that caring for an ailing husband is far worse than nursing a sick child.

For the most part we kept silent about my husband's illnesses, thinking that was the best policy to follow. Now I wonder if that was also a mistake. Had we been more open about his afflictions, perhaps the people would have understood and rallied to our support; yet we did what we thought best at the time.

During this period we also struggled with still another unnerving problem. Unfortunately the parsonage had been built too near a river. When the water table rose, the basement flooded, threatening the furnace and the water pump which served both the church and parsonage. We lived apprehensively for months on end lest the sump pump stop working and the water rise and ruin these expensive systems. When this happened at three o'clock one morning, we had to call church men to come and help bail water.

The stress and strain of those many months took a toll of my physical strength also. I honestly wondered, after a time, if life would ever change for the better. Would it be like this for the rest of my existence? That year when spring arrived I was so exhausted I felt I could not possibly clean that rambling old house.

"O Lord, send help," I petitioned, never imagining how He would answer.

After the furnace had been inundated by water several times, corrosion resulted, and when the repairmen came to fix it, their efforts sent greasy ebon soot soaring throughout the house.

That was the living end! I had had it! For all those long months I kept smiling, refusing to complain despite the intense tension I was undergoing. But now I fought desperately to hold back the tears. My strength was utterly gone. I had no heart or energy to cope with the ugly mess.

Then the miracle!

"How about our insurance?" I asked suddenly, as if by inspiration. "Wouldn't it take care of having the house cleaned?"

Happily it did. Professional cleaners washed down the walls and shampooed the carpeting. Draperies, bedspreads, and many of our clothes came back from the laundry fresh and soot-free. In spite of the initial trauma, the end result was well worth the suffering. For once, someone else did my spring cleaning for me.

God does move in mysterious ways His wonders to perform.

* * *

So much happened and so many people had left our ranks that my husband seriously questioned the advisability of continuing his pastoral stay in that assignment. There was also the matter of his health to be considered. Perhaps he should take an earlier than usual retirement from the active ministry.

For months we prayed, earnestly seeking for guidance. That, as I have previously mentioned, was nothing new. No move was ever made without first waiting before the Lord for direction.

After fervent prayer and much contemplation, Buddy decided to follow the method used by our denomination to determine the placement—or replacement—of pastors. He would submit to the decision of the church members, letting God work through them to reveal His will to us.

"Why are you doing this today?" Judy asked, surprised.

But I thought little of her astonishment—until later. What did she know then that I didn't?

I had planned a parsonage breakfast for the ladies on the day before the members were to register their vote concerning their pastor. Regardless of what anyone may have thought, there was absolutely no political intent involved in my action. This simply was something I had planned to do for quite some time. Because of known impending circumstances, it seemed to be now or never. Had I been aware of the unknown, it probably would have been the latter. Be that as it may, I acted out of love and have never regretted the outlay of energy and expense.

Moreover, my husband and I both sought diligently for God's will to be done and had promised Him we would accept whatever came. In fact, we had even gone so far as to pray, "O Lord, if You want us to leave, let us know it—if it means being voted out."

Still, that seemed unlikely. Although we had sensed an indescribable aura for some time, the people had never openly expressed antagonism toward us, nor had they been nasty and disagreeable. We often wondered at their aloofness, but we had no inkling they collectively felt the same about us.

We learned, years later, how individuals in a former assignment had been faithful in doing their visitation work, using it as an opportunity to campaign against the pastor. Was that true here? Or did these folk "let their fingers do the walking"?

Whatever . . . that matters little. The important thing is, the Lord answered our prayers. And that's quite a story.

But first . . .

15

Deliverance

I am a genuine homebody at heart. I confess I am vastly different from the majority of modern-day women. My home is my castle, and therein I am content.

I love houses. All kinds. They intrigue me. When we drive by lighted homes at night and the curtains are open, I am a first-class Peeping Tom.

As a child I loved playhouses. Now my husband accuses me of "playing house" when I rearrange the furniture, plants, and knickknacks.

All my adult life I yearned for a home of our own. Shack or shanty—that mattered little. A converted chicken house would have suited me fine. Therefore, if there was any sacrifice for me in the pastoral ministry, it was being unable to live in our own home. Nevertheless, I must also confess that throughout the years I thoroughly enjoyed turning every parsonage, whatever its description, into a livable dwelling place. Sometimes it was a real challenge.

One of our earliest parsonages was at least 100 years old—a converted (what else for a preacher to live in?) store building. The huge and drafty monstrosity sat smack on Main Street next to the fire station. And it seemed that most of the fires occurred on Saturday nights.

Because of the size and antiquity of the building, the upstairs' rooms were frightening to our little girls. Nor could I blame the children for feeling insecure. The room in which they slept was approximately 14 feet by 20 feet, and the shadows that fell on its walls gave even an adult an eerie sensation. A crude closet, opening off the room, served as a connector to the attic of the adjacent church building. All this contributed to the effluvium of a haunted house.

Downstairs, the dining room floor sagged so perceptibly, I humorously declared you had to shift into second gear to get from the front room to the kitchen, which sported a worn-out sink and practically no cupboards. The window-panes were old and stained by the years. The floors, made of wide boards, were full of splinters.

A bright linoleum did wonders for the swayed dining room floor, however. And by placing our table and chairs in the middle of the room, we used the space to advantage. A crocheted doily, edged in rose, plus colorful plastic draperies added pleasing touches.

For the living room, a used rug which matched the deep red of the sofa and chair was obtained at a bargain price. When everything was in place, including pictures on the walls, the grotesque manse became quite an attractive domain.

Likewise, each parsonage that followed, although none ever exceeded this one in age, became a challenge. One facet about moving frequently which I thoroughly enjoyed was the opportunity to vent my creative urge on a variety of houses.

Paint and decals have worked wonders on odds and ends of furniture. Unbleached muslin has attractively covered many windows. And houseplants have added a homey touch. Turning houses into homes has always been a pleasure for me.

While living in parsonages, we felt little concern about where we would reside when we reached retirement age. Jesus promised, "Seek ye first the kingdom of God, and his righteousness; and all these things shall be added unto you"

(Matt. 6:33). And we simply believed He would provide, somehow, when the time came.

But after Buddy's health failed, we realized that faith and works go together. It was time to *do* something about the future. Let's be practical: The Lord helps those who help themselves. Facing up to the bald truth, we realized that no one was going to look out for us when we were too old or infirm to continue dwelling in parsonages. Common sense told us we should begin putting feet to our prayers. Immediately. The mid-50s did not allow an overabundance of time to fritter away daydreaming or indulging in wishful thinking.

By dent of a few business transactions, diligent saving, and a gift from my parents, we had accumulated a small nest egg. Moreover, we had obtained a parcel of land a few years before which was now free of debt. On this acreage we intended to build a house and live out our sunset years in view of the nearby lake.

Now the pressure was on. Fantasy must bow to factuality. So we decided to use what money we had, obtain a loan, have a house built, and then rent it out until we needed to move into it ourselves. The rental fee would take care of the payments. This seemed the only way to go.

Thus, we began praying diligently and investigating the possibilities. After querying a carpenter or two, we received a call from a contractor in the area where our land was located. He had heard we were interested in building and offered to put up a house for us at such a ridiculously low price, we felt we could not turn him down. So we signed the contract, rejoicing over the way the Lord was answering our petitions.

Immediately we set about to apply for a loan. The first bank turned us down because of our contractor, they said. But we were so excited about getting a home of our own, we weren't on the outlook for negative news. Therefore, we gave it little thought.

119

A second bank turned us down for the same reason. Still we failed to catch on.

At the third one we found the people more cooperative. At least the lady in charge of the loan department pleasantly assisted us in making application.

Because the deal seemed to be a settled affair, we gave the contractor two checks, amounting to over $900, enabling him to begin excavating within days.

How exciting! What fun it was picking out colors, carpeting, and countertop, and drawing plans.

On Wednesday the telephone rang.

"This is Mrs. Brown at the State Savings Bank," the caller said. "You're not going to like what you're going to hear. I took your application in, and they turned you down on your loan. It isn't your fault. It's your contractor."

Our next move was to report this turn of events to him.

"I'm shocked," he responded. "I've done a lot of business with those people. I certainly do not understand this."

Before hanging up he promised to do some investigating and return our call shortly.

For safety's sake, Buddy immediately contacted our local bank and stopped payment on the checks we had already given Mr. Carson—just in case he wasn't what we had thought. But surely this was an answer to our prayer for a house. Virgil Carson had to be trustworthy. Sitting at our kitchen table, telling about the well-known Bible school he had attended, talking about the Lord and his activity in his church, he had inspired our utmost confidence. Yet . . .

Monday morning Mr. Carson called twice. He explained how anxious he was to help us get a home. Surely we could find a way to make financial arrangements. We agreed to meet him the next day and explore more possibilities.

In the meantime we continued to pray, leaving the consequences with the Lord. And our absolute trust brought peace.

About 10:30 that night the telephone rang once more. I answered it downstairs.

"This is Mr. Waldo of the State Savings Bank. I've been trying to get you."

"We've been away all afternoon."

"I must inform you at the start that this conversation is being taped. I'm calling to apologize for turning you down on your loan."

"Just a moment." I handed my husband the telephone and scurried up the steps to listen in on the extension. After we both were on the line, the caller began again.

"Rev. Spray, this is Mr. Waldo of the State Savings Bank. First, I want to make it clear to you that this conversation is being recorded."

We waited. How unusual!

"I want to apologize for turning you down on your loan. Mr. Carson's lawyer contacted me today. We certainly don't want to get involved in a defamation of character suit over this."

"Well, I think we have just about decided to drop the deal," Buddy replied. "We gave Mr. Carson a couple of checks to begin excavating the basement, but I called the bank and put a hold on them."

"Oh, I'm so sorry!" exclaimed the caller. "I wish you hadn't done that. I surely think we can work something out. Mr. Carson is a good man, and we don't want to get into any trouble with him over this."

"Do you really think he is trustworthy?"

"Yes! Certainly he is! He's a good man and we have done a lot of business with him. We want your business, too. You don't even have to come in to apply for a commitment loan. It's already being processed and will be in the mail in 7 to 10 days."

My, you sure sound like Mr. Carson, I thought.

121

"Do you think it is safe then for us to turn over the rest of our money to Mr. Carson tomorrow?"

"Absolutely! There's not a thing in the world to worry about. We want your business. We'll see that you get a loan. Mr. Carson is a good customer of ours. He has been doing business with us for a long time."

"You're really sure we are safe in doing this? You should know."

"Yes, I'd advise you to get on with it right away. Go down there tomorrow and get this thing moving. It's a good deal for you. This house will retail for much more than Mr. Carson is offering to build it. You're getting it at a greatly reduced price. I'd do it. Get it started while the weather is nice."

"You certainly are encouraging."

"Mr. Carson has been working with us for 15 years. We're so sorry we pulled this boner. He has built many homes." Was someone holding a gun to the caller's back?

He was so urgent it made one wonder. "This is on tape, as I said, and I have agreed to send a copy to Mr. Carson's lawyer."

"Would you mind sending us a copy, too?"

"I'm sorry but only two will be made. Nevertheless, one will be available to you in case you ever need it."

"We are to meet Mr. Carson tomorrow morning at 10. If you will give us a loan, it looks like we can go ahead with our plans."

"Good! I'm sure you won't be sorry."

"The Lord really is working it out," we exclaimed jubilantly as we hung up the receivers. "Isn't it wonderful!"

But the Holy Spirit whispered, "It wouldn't hurt to call the bank in the morning and ask for Mr. Waldo before you meet your contractor."

And we decided to do just that. After coffee, Buddy used the pay phone at the restaurant to dial the State Savings Bank. "Could I speak to Mr. Waldo, please?" he asked.

"We have no one working here by that name."

"Are you sure? He called us last night."

"There is no Mr. Waldo working here. Let me put you in contact with someone else."

Further inquiry substantiated that. However, Waldo was the first name of one of the vice presidents.

"Thank you," Buddy said. By then we both knew that the call the night before had been a hoax. Who could have known all the private details of the transaction? Excepting Mr. Carson?

"It had to be him! I can't believe it!"

"You know, I thought last night, You sure sound like Mr. Carson, but I didn't say it."

"We still have to meet him."

How we wanted to wake up and find it all a bad dream! Nevertheless, we were not asleep. We were wide-awake. Nor were we watching a dramatic television program. We were living a whopper of a mystery story—and it was scarey! Mighty scarey! The man we had to face knew we were bringing a check for several thousand dollars. Would he try to take it by force? Anyone who would perpetrate such a farce as that phone call might try anything.

"We won't say a word to him about the call last night," we agreed, "until we get to the bank."

While we waited in the prearranged location, we prayed as if our lives depended on it—and perhaps they did. When Mr. Carson arrived, he quickly approached us, anxious to talk business.

"Would you mind going with us to the bank to see about the loan?" my husband asked.

"I'd be more than happy to do so," he replied congenially. "I should have sent you to the man I usually deal with. I don't know his last name, but his first name is Waldo. We need to get this loan through right away because I'd like to begin work on the house while the weather is nice."

123

There were the two telltale pieces—"Waldo" and "while the weather is nice." They exactly fitted the puzzle. Both echoed the conversation of the night before.

We followed as Mr. Carson led the way to the bank—prayerfully, excitedly, anxiously. We were in the very throes of a real-life drama. It was unbelievable.

At the bank we waited in the reception area until the vice president named Waldo was free to speak to us. Then the contractor rushed pell-mell into his office, a nervous wreck.

It didn't take Buddy long to tell about the telephone call we had received the night before, being careful not to make any accusations.

When I summoned enough courage to look at Mr. Carson, he was slumped in a chair, looking for all the world like death. Still, he managed to throw in a few remarks now and then, keeping up his game of charades. "I don't blame you for being concerned," he said. "I've had funny things happen to me, but this is the strangest."

While we discussed the entire story, the implications and possible accruements, fully aware of the offender's presence, he unflinchingly kept up his masquerade. How close he came to having a heart attack only the Lord knows.

Returning to the bank a bit later, we asked "Mr. Waldo" in private, "Would you go through with this deal if you were in our place?"

"No!" he replied emphatically. "Not if I lost my $900."

Fortunately, we were successful in retrieving our checks. When we learned later that Mr. Carson went bankrupt soon after that distressing encounter, several of our questions were automatically answered.

It wasn't easy to watch the promise of a home long hoped for go down the drain. Nevertheless, we rejoiced with exceeding great joy. It pays to heed the Spirit's promptings. God worked another miracle in our lives, delivering us from financial disaster. Furthermore, He had something better in store for us.

16

The Panacea

It was an early August afternoon. Overhead, huge puffs of cotton hovered motionless in the northern expanse of sky. I sat on the back steps snapping green beans for canning. While my fingers moved rapidly, my mind took flight. How true were the words of the apostle Paul: "Now unto him that is able to do exceeding abundantly above all that we ask or think . . . be glory" (Eph. 3:20-21).

When we first met long ago in that lowly country church, neither Buddy nor I dreamed of the things the Lord had in store for us. Sometimes the pickings have been pretty lean, but God has answered many prayers and supplied our needs—plenteously. And our requests certainly have been varied.

* * *

One of the privileges of living in the parsonage is entertaining such honored guests as missionaries, evangelists, and church dignitaries.

I confess, however, that this has sometimes been an exhausting experience, especially in the earlier years. I used to scrub the house from top to bottom, feeling like our guests had the facility to see into the remotest corners.

I should have realized that the greatest people are the humblest. This surely was true of Dr. Deen, whom we dearly loved. No matter where he was, or to whom he was talking, he put himself out to speak to our daughters, a gesture we deeply appreciated.

When entertaining company, one naturally seeks to put his best foot (and food) forward. Therefore, my prayer list has contained requests for dishes and silverware. A pretty table is perhaps as important as good food. At least it makes up for a lack of culinary skill many times.

God sent manna from heaven to feed the Israelites. He sent us coupons via the grocery store, premiums via gas stations, and Christmas gifts to provide an attractive table for our guests.

We waited many more years for china, crystal, and our 1847 Rogers, but Dr. Deen was especially attracted to our inexpensive flatware. When he commented on its resemblance to sterling, I exclaimed, "Brother Deen, I got this silverware by saving coupons from Kellogg's cereal packages."

"I don't care," he replied. "I still think it is pretty."

When the girls grew older, they discussed who would get the Kellogg set with the monogrammed S. What if her married name began with another letter?

"The S could stand for sin," I overheard one remark, jokingly.

"Or salvation," suggested the other.

Years later, Sue got the faithful set because she did not change her last initial. Sybil traded her S for M.

Money received from a congregation on our 25th anniversary enabled us to purchase the Rogers set. The Christmas gift from another congregation helped us procure china from Montgomery Ward. And again, trading stamps were exchanged for crystal.

During Assignment 3 the Lord supplied another temporal need even before we asked Him.

Shortly after moving in, we redecorated the parsonage. Since the dining and kitchen areas were separated by a wide arch, we used complementary colors—a soft green for the dining room and a rather shocking shade of pink for the kitchen. Accents of black did a nice job of making the rooms attractive.

But, oh, how we needed a rug for the dining room floor. Even by placing the table in the middle of the room and arranging the rest of the furniture just right, the bare spots were all too conspicuous. Yet we simply had to make the best of it. There was no money for new linoleum, much less a woolen rug.

One warm Sunday evening several of our relatives came to visit. After the service, we had them in for a cool drink. While squeezing lemons and measuring sugar, we chatted.

Suddenly my cousin said, "I have a rug at home that just about matches your kitchen."

"Oh!" I looked a bit shocked. Was she right? Honestly, I had wondered if we had been a bit too daring in selecting the color we had chosen.

"You may have it if you want it."

"Are you kidding?"

"No, I'm not kidding! I'll give it to you. I bought it a while ago to put in my bedroom, but afterward I found out the state won't let me use it—on account of my patients. All my floors have to be washable."

"Well . . . that . . ."

"Something told me, 'I have a place for it and will tell you where it belongs later on.' So I put it in the attic and waited."

"How large is it?" I finally ventured. Surely she was talking about a throw rug.

"It's 9 by 12, I believe."

I squealed with delight.

The next morning we went after the rug. When we got it home, we could scarcely believe our eyes. It matched the kitchen walls perfectly. In fact, we could not have done a better job color wise if we had shopped for it specifically.

What a miracle! God is so good. I would have gladly opted for a linoleum, but the Lord had something better for us.

*   *   *

He undertook for us in a rather strange (and perhaps amusing) way during a later assignment. We had moved from a small parsonage into a much larger one and needed more furniture to fill up the additional space.

At a local store the salesman asked, "Just what kind of sofa are you looking for?"

I glanced around the showroom and almost immediately my eyes rested on a couch directly to our left. "Something like this would do," I answered boldly, knowing the price was more than we could afford.

"Well, let's see," he said thoughtfully. "We can allow you $150 for your refrigerator." (This church furnished the appliance, so we were disposing of ours.) When he added the amount of needed cash to complete the transaction, we were dazed. Besides giving us a generous allowance for our used refrigerator, the man was knocking off another substantial discount from the marked price. And the difference—it was exactly the amount our former church had given us for a farewell gift.

I could scarcely believe our good fortune. The avocado of the sofa would beautifully compliment the soft gold carpeting in our "new" parsonage. It was large, spacious enough to help fill the space in the ample-sized living room. And the design? The very thing to go with our antiques and "glorified junk."

But the end was not yet. We were to discover anew the truth of Rom. 8:28.

We enjoyed living in that parsonage. It was an older house, but it was comfortable and cozy. Because of the size, the two of us seldom used the living room when we were

alone. Much of the time I kept the draperies closed. Therefore, when the sofa began to fade, I was certain the sunlight
wasn't to blame. With disbelief we watched our lovely couch
turn into what at first appeared to be an unusually odd and
unattractive color.

I felt sick.

Contacting the store manager, he promised to write the
manufacturer. When we didn't hear, I called again. And
again. At last we were informed that the company would
allow us $50.00 for the damage. We accepted the allowance,
applying it on the purchase of a needed chair—in soft gold.

Then we were called to another church. When I knew
we were moving into a parsonage that had antique gold carpeting, I grew concerned. How would our faded sofa look
against that floor covering?

Miraculously by the time we moved, our sofa had faded
evenly and to just the right shade, allowing it to blend perfectly with the hard-to-match carpeting. And the chair? It,
too, harmonized as well as if it had been specifically chosen
for the room. Also, the slipcover on the second chair contained exactly the same shade of gold as the rug.

Did God know when, much to our regret, we had to
dispose of our like-new refrigerator that we would need the
price to purchase a sofa that would eventually fade? And
make us happy in doing so?

Of course He knew! This experience added to our reservoir of trust, trust which enables us to hold steady when the
unrecognizable is in the process of being harmoniously
blended together for our good and God's glory.

*   *   *

The Lord also worked miracles where the girls' educations were concerned. Many women go to work and pay their
children's way through college. And I confess I have sometimes felt guilty because I didn't. Nevertheless, I had to live

with my own conscience and I just didn't feel it was the Lord's will for me to work outside our home. If my decision worked hardships on our children, I am sorry. However, I can honestly say I did what I believed was God's will for me. And He took care of the rest.

Although our older daughter finished college after her marriage, both the girls came through with better educations than we had hoped.

Furthermore, since both our daughters are now women of beautiful and staunch character, perhaps the struggle and sacrifice helped fit them for the challenges they face today.

* * *

Another wonderful miracle happened not long after Sybil was married and living in a college town. Wayne and she had just moved out of their mobile home into an apartment.

While listening to a weather report, my husband heard the reporter say a tornado was headed into the direction of the town where our children lived. Without wasting any time, he set out for the basement where he often went to pray. There he asked the Lord to lift or turn the tornado.

On our way to prayer meeting that night we listened to the news on the car radio. The tornado had struck the college, hitting the administration building where Sybil was working on the first floor. But my husband had received such definite assurance from the Lord that he confidently told the people, "She will be all right."

Back home we tried unsuccessfully to reach the children. Finally, they got through to us. Sybil was safe and sound. The Lord had lifted the tornado two stories, taking the third. Fortunately, there were no fatalities. Only one or two injuries were reported, but the mobile home in which our children had been living until a few days before was demolished.

*   *   *

Someone has said that prayer is the most important task of the preacher's wife. It is the true remedy for her many ills, the panacea for countless difficulties. Unless she learns to talk to God, she certainly cannot make it successfully. Much less be contented and happy. Nor can anyone else, for that matter.

Prayer has resolved many problems for us across the years. It has brought not only the warm, reassuring touch of the Holy Spirit to our own hearts, but it has also brought salvation to those who were sincerely searching for peace of mind and heart.

Prayer has brought many answers—healing for mental and physical disturbances, protection, silverware, china, furniture, college educations, eyeglasses, clothing, housing, solutions to lovers' quarrels, typewriters, rugs, inspirations, secretarial assistance . . . ad infinitum.

Prayer has been our panacea for every assignment. What a thrill it is to know that the source of God's supply has not diminished. The more we ask, the more He shall supply. And the bigger the challenge, the greater the miracle!

And prayer would bring us a home when it was needed.

Before we go further, however, there is something I'd like to set straight . . .

17

"Regular Lady"

While his mother and I chatted gaily, Jamie fixed himself a bowl of oatmeal and some hot chocolate, filling the cup so full it nearly ran over.

"Now I want to know," he asked abruptly.

"What is it, Jamie?" I countered, both surprised and amused.

"Is your husband a preacher, or are you a regular lady?"

"Well, Jamie, it's like this: My husband is a preacher, but I am a 'regular' lady, too."

Are there others like Jamie? Do they also wonder if preachers' wives are "regular" people? It just happens that the spouses of the latter are employed by congregations instead of General Motors, the county road commission, or Uncle Sam.

Yes, preachers' wives are very human. They brush their teeth, mash potatoes, clean up after sloppy kids, and do the other things "regular" women do. Yet theirs is a unique lifestyle, one with its own set of blessings—and tensions.

While serving an early assignment, the village doctor told me, "All the preachers' wives who come here have physical problems."

Psychosomatic ailments are common to both ministers and their wives. Stress and strain take an extravagant toll of physical, mental, and emotional health.

A pastor suffers from professional pressures—meeting goals, raising money, pushing programs, and coping with, all too often, an authority-resistant clientele. But the tensions with which his spouse must cope may be doubled—or tripled.

First, like everyone else, she must deal with her own personal infirmities, conflicts, inadequacies, and limitations.

Second, she is her husband's shock absorber, his tranquilizing potion, his pep pill or downer, whichever is needed at the moment, his lover, and the mother of his runny-nosed, diaper-clad, colicky offspring.

Third, being a mother in a parsonage often calls for double-strength fortitude. Preachers' kids must live as normally as possible in a less than normal atmosphere. Dwelling in a glass house without breaking panes (literally as well as figuratively) can be a nerve-tingling experience.

Fourth, she is a sounding board for the congregation. A go-between for pastor and people. Many complaints reach her ears in an effort to get through to the preacher's.

Naturally, many tensions endured by the clerical couple cannot be aired publicly. Therefore, good communication between them is vitally important. Verbal expression is good for the body as well as the soul; it expels poisons and brings healing. Two heads are better than one, we're told. Furthermore, sharing creates an invincible bond between two people.

Certainly I, too, have suffered many tensions while living in the parsonage. Nevertheless, since I am naturally susceptible to tension, I'm quite sure I would have suffered stress wherever we lived or whatever other profession my husband may have followed.

I wish I could say I have been the ideal preacher's wife, a model of decorum, but I haven't. I freely confess that I have goofed all too many times—laughed in the wrong places; talked too much, oftentimes unwisely; rushed pell-mell into action when I should have waited. Not that I didn't try. In fact, I probably tried too hard to do everything right, but I am human and therefore subject to many errors. In the beginning, especially, I strove for perfection and was doomed to failure.

I shall never forget the first ministers' wives' retreat I attended. I came away totally depressed and remained that way for months. Having endeavored to be a paragon of virtue, I was genuinely discouraged to find how far short of perfection I came in spite of my intense efforts to the contrary.

After grappling long enough with this elusive goal, I decided that anyone who halfway succeeds in life must learn to be himself. He must accept the fact that there is no way he can please everyone, try as he may. Ask any politician.

We hadn't been in one of our assignments long before we began hearing critical remarks about a former pastor's wife.

"She dressed like a fashion plate."

"She was really snazzy."

Now I know this gal and her husband hovered close to the poverty level, but she had a flare for style and was a gifted seamstress. She remodeled many of her garments, expertly fashioning them into attractive creations. Furthermore, she had a figure that could do justice to an ample-sized dishrag.

All this brought to my mind another pastor's wife I once knew. The entire congregation was embarrassed to introduce her to strangers because of her careless appearance.

Putting it all together, I came to this conclusion: If you please some people, you automatically displease others. And vice versa. I decided from then on to do my best to please Jesus. If I pleased Him, perhaps I would please the majority of the people. That became the standard by which I since have lived.

Preachers' wives should want to look nice and have pretty clothes—like everyone else. Personally, I prefer a few quality items to many cheap pieces. But neatness should be a woman's prime concern.

I confess that keeping up with the latest styles doesn't bother me, however. Having grown up during the depression, I learned early to make the best of what we could afford, or what was given to me, or to do without.

Moreover, shortness and chubbiness never contribute effectively to one's becoming the most chic madame.

My personal acquaintances certainly can testify that everything they have seen me wear hasn't been as becoming as I wish it had been. I was wearing a "marked down" item when I passed a couple of women on my way to play the piano.

"That dress makes her look pudgier than ever," I overheard one whisper to the other.

Hats were my weakness before the days of bouffant hairstyles. For years I never appeared in church on Sunday morning without one.

"Bess said you wore your hat the wrong way," Nell confided to me one day. "But I told her, 'Mrs. Spray knows the right way to wear her hat!'"

As I think about that bonnet-type hat now, Bess may have been right. If so, the saleslady gave me the wrong pitch. Thank the dear Lord for a sense of humor. It has saved many a day.

My husband was instrumental in leading Ross to the Lord and getting him involved in the church. From the very start we recognized that this handsome lad was gifted. When he professed to be called to preach, we rejoiced, and as always Buddy tried to help him, urging him to prepare properly.

But Ross wanted to be an instant bishop. Instead of attending valuable classes, he importantly strutted around the church with his Bible under his arm.

As much as I detested Ross's desire for prestige without paying the price, I must confess there came a time when I realized I was somewhat like him. I enjoyed the glamour of being a minister's wife but not the part that called for self-denial and sacrifice. Sometimes it was easier to receive love than reciprocate it.

Numerous books extol the jollies of being a preacher's wife (and there are many!). But all of life in the parsonage is not a bowl of cherries. Nor even fun. Realistically speaking, a call to serve is also a call to sacrifice. When we of our free will say yes to a divine calling, we are choosing a life of sacrifice, whether we recognize it or not. That doesn't tickle the funny bone!

This goes for money and material possessions. The clergy should never try to compete with the laity when it comes to accumulating wealth. They should not expect to live on as high a plane (even though it appeals to their appetites) as their most affluent members. If a preacher insists on owning every luxury he sees his members possess, he is doomed for disappointment. Perhaps he should seek for more lucrative employment.

The parsonage family must also sacrifice their time. I have minimized phone calls by deliberately setting the right example, seldom calling anyone unless it pertained to church business. In addition to that, I have let people know I was busy—and they have respected my forthrightness.

Some people who have little to do themselves forget that a pastor's wife has many, many others clamoring for her attention also. One such person used to call and talk by the hour, hoping I would let my husband know how mistreated and unappreciated she was.

Sybil said she mopped the entire kitchen floor while listening to a parishioner one day. Fortunately, she had a long cord on her phone, an essential in every parsonage.

And while I'm at it, I may as well confess that missionary workdays have always been a trial to me. Not that I am unsympathetic toward the work of world missions, but spending all day over quilting frames is not my idea of fun when I have a lot to do at home. Plus that, I invariably end up feeling defeated. Did I talk too much? Did I say the wrong thing? Why didn't I keep my mouth closed like a prim and proper preacher's wife should?

Physical strength must be sacrificed ofttimes, too. Visiting a chronic complainer when you need to be in bed yourself calls for a special portion of divine grace.

Nevertheless, God's love constrains and sustains those who give themselves to Him unconditionally. Jesus Christ made the supreme sacrifice. It is therefore only reasonable that we, in turn, present ourselves to Him as living sacrifices, to be used by Him in any way He chooses. One day His "Well done" will more than compensate for any self-denial we have made here below.

*   *   *

As you may have guessed, I was not the quiet, retiring person a minister's wife is so often pictured to be. I could not remain submerged, *terra incognita*, in the nursery or church kitchen. No matter how hard I tried to stay out of public view, I invariably found myself in the limelight. If a piano player was missing, I was substituting. If a teacher was needed, soon I was standing before a class. My husband is the quieter (and wiser) and more phlegmatic. I am quick and impulsive. Therefore, I was overly prone to take the initiative, often ill-advisedly, occasionally to my regret.

Frankly, I admire the silent type of preacher's wife, and I have often wished to be more like my mother, who humbly accepted the menial tasks, subserviently waiting on others.

It took me a long time to realize that all women are not like Ma. Nor are all men like Dad. Quite often the temperaments and personality types of couples are the reverse. And I happen (or God ordained it) to inherit some of my father's choleric tendencies—and a bit of his uniqueness and creativity, too.

Also, as the eldest of seven children, I learned to shoulder responsibility early in life. This conditioning naturally lapsed over into our marriage and the church. Truthfully, it probably has been a curse rather than a blessing at times, for I have accepted obligations which would have been better off relinquished to others.

Furthermore, possessing personal doubts and fears and a strong sense of rightness and wrongness, I was easily influenced by authoritarian influences. Early in our ministry an older pastor said, "Look after him now. See that he does what he's supposed to do." Now I believe that the man meant it facetiously and that I took his statement too much to heart, but that injunction left an indelible imprint on my mind—one that was hard to throw. When reality did not measure up to the mental images I had created, I felt defeated and chagrined. I confess it took me many years to accept my husband's professional uniqueness.

Buddy is a born nonconformist. When it is suggested to him that he do something in a certain way, he instantly begins figuring out another means of getting the job done. Instead of being coerced into doing it the "right way," he is instantly challenged to do it the "wrong way"—successfully. This can be a valuable trait at times, but it can also create tension for a perfectionist like myself.

Not only did he refuse to stay in the church office alone for hours on end, he got his sermons in an armchair at home—under my feet. (Fortunately, I might add, the knees, not the seat, of his pants were the first to go, but that was because he sat with his legs crossed.)

My persistent efforts to change Buddy caused tensions for us both. I worried constantly about what people would think, what they would say, and the possible repercussions his unconventionality might accrue. But my concern only added to his determination to do it his own way. And my protectiveness created stress for me.

Finally, I surrendered my husband completely to God. I promised to stop trying to mother him, to let God use him in His own way—whatever happened. After all, He was responsible. Didn't He fashion each of us in the first place?

The Lord made me as I am, choleric traits and all. He created Buddy as he is. When I fail to accept either one of our personal uniquenesses, I am thwarting His divine plan and purpose. I expect to be accepted "just as I am." Likewise, I am obligated to do the same where others are concerned, including my husband. Actually, I eventually came to look on our differences as a plus, not a minus. By complementing each other, we are enabled to do twice as much for Jesus.

Although I confess that having a man around the house much of the time can be nerve-racking, I wouldn't think of forfeiting the special closeness we have always enjoyed.

Many preachers and their wives drift apart. This ought not to be—for any couple. Isn't it the woman's responsibility to keep her husband so interested at home he will not want to look elsewhere? If she does her part to add fuel to their romance, she will not have to be overly concerned about the aggressive women he encounters. (Of course, there are exceptions to every rule.) And like death and taxes, women who flaunt themselves are always with professional men. Doctors, lawyers, and ministers especially hold fascination for many members of the opposite sex. Perhaps women look upon them as surrogate fathers, would-be lovers, or understanding husbands, according to their individual emotional needs. Or it could be that professional men represent greater challenges. As our moral fiber continues to weaken, it is sad but true that more and more of God's chosen are falling into the clutches of wives of Potiphar and daughters-in-law of Judah.

Women will get crushes on their pastors whether or not the men give them the least bit of encouragement. Any preacher's wife who has a handsome, appealing husband can rest assured he will be the recipient of many approving glances.

Quite frankly, I have always felt my husband outdid me in the looks department. Perhaps the Lord knew I needed a handsome husband to help boost my own sagging ego, to give me the confidence I sorely needed. But I, too, had something to offer him.

Fortunately, what a wife lacks in physical pulchritude, she can make up for in other ways. She can give a man the affection, sympathy, admiration, understanding, undergirding, physical love, and moral strength he needs to conquer the world. And a preacher's wife may be called upon to double up on these potions.

Certainly another of the preacher's wife's greatest concerns is the welfare of her children. In *How to Live with Less Tension* I wrote about the time I decided to do a bit of research.

"Sybil, how do you feel about being a preacher's child?" I asked when she came in from school.

"I hardly realize that I am one," she replied.

"Why were you an hour late tonight?"

"I had to stay in for talking during class."

That convinced me she was "regular," too.

Ofttimes a pastor's wife is faced with the question: Shall I hurt my children or arouse the displeasure of a parishioner?

140

Sybil was getting her first heels for Christmas, and she oozed with anticipation and delight. After all, this was a major plateau in the life of a brand-new teenager.

I had made her a beautiful navy dress of flocked nylon (then in vogue), trimmed with lace, to wear with her new patent pumps to the Christmas program.

A few days before the big event, Brother Stinson, the father of several girls, came to me on the verge of tears. "Please don't let Sybil wear her heels Sunday. My girls are giving me fits to buy them heels, too."

I was dumbfounded. How was I to cope with this one? After all, my child had been living for the occasion. Was it right to deny her her moment of glory because a father refused to grant his children their requests—whatever the reason? Both he and his wife worked, so surely it wasn't the matter of money. Or was it?

All this threw me into a real quandary. Certainly I didn't want to hurt this good, sensitive man. On the other hand, how could I possibly disappoint my child?

That time my mother heart won out. My child's happiness had to come first.

Parsonage parents are faced with other difficult decisions, too. A child must be taught the principles of unprejudiced and impartial love. This, however, can lead to still another problem. How do you teach a child to "love without dissimulation" and at the same time instill within him lofty ideals? How do you teach a 10-year-old to love everyone he meets and at 20 to look for a life partner who is of the highest moral fiber and social caliber? This calls for much prayer, tact, and divinely imparted wisdom. However, this dilemma confronts not only ministers but laymen as well.

Perhaps, again, the theory of loving without especially liking must be applied. While Jesus loved every individual He met, He had a few special friends whom He chose as companions. Doesn't He allow us the same privilege?

Many believe a preacher and his wife should never discuss church-related problems within hearing distance of their children. No doubt many should not. If their children are compulsive talkers, they had better refrain—or move. But I confess we never made it a policy to withhold everything from our girls. After all, they had eyes, ears, and brains. They were observant, intelligent, and sensitive. Why lead them to believe the church was Utopia when it wasn't? Personally, we thought it best for them to face up to reality and handle life's problems with prayer and faith. Besides, our children knew that what was said within their hearing was spoken without malicious intent.

If parents carry chips on their shoulders, they should remain silent. But love covers a multitude of sins, stresses, and situations. It makes a difference in *what* one says, *how* one says it, *when* he says it, *where* he says it, and *why* he says it.

Children need to feel a sense of belonging. The greater a part in the ministry the children feel, the easier it is to accept their share of the responsibility. Our little granddaughter had the right idea when she said, "Everyone wants *us*."

*   *   *

In a technical sense, the church calls the minister. But in another sense, the church also calls his wife and children. That's because they come as a package deal. Like strawberries and cream. Or johnnycake and milk. The spouse and kids are not merely tacked-on accessories. They are an inseparable unit. And very "regular."

A teenager once told me, "You're the first preacher's wife I ever saw who was human." And it pleased me no end.

18

At Home

Following our upsetting and near catastrophic experience with Mr. Carson, we gave up on the idea of building a house on our land. Perhaps we should look for something already built, we decided. If we could find a house in need of repairs, requiring only a small down payment, we could renovate it. Then we could rent it out until we needed to move into it ourselves.

Having observed the plight of many older people, we concluded it would be best to live in a small town or city, within walking distance of stores, church, and professional services, when the time for retirement arrived.

Toward the end of the year Buddy ran across an ad in the area newspaper. The house was located in a quiet little city not too far away. It sounded like something we could handle.

On a frigid November day when the ground was wearing a thin blanket of snow, we pulled up in front of the frame structure. And at first sight of it, a warm sensation welled up within me.

"This is it!" something seemed to say.

Moreover, the location was ideal, exactly what we had in mind. A supermarket was just around the corner. Professional offices and a church were not much more than a stone's throw away.

The real estate salesman was waiting outside in the cold. He had advertised an open house showing but had been unable to contact the owner. The occupants were nowhere in sight—or in town.

"I can't get inside," he explained, shivering. "I'm sorry I can't show it to you. No one knows where the owner has gone."

So we returned home disappointed. Days passed with no further word. Still, we were interested.

Finally, a friend who is also in real estate obtained a key and took us to look over the place. A first glance told us plainly that the one who lived here was unquestionably interested in something other than housekeeping.

However, the price was attractive. In fact, it was below Mr. Carson's shockingly low offer to build. Only 13 years old, this house offered the same area space, and it was set in an ample-sized yard with trees.

Of course there was a lot to do before it was livable. Each room screamed for paint. Bare floors in the bedrooms begged for covering. The kitchen carpet was blackened by grease, and the bathroom carpeting also needed replacing.

Several features were especially enticing, nevertheless. For instance, one bedroom could double as a study. The west wall was the very thing for a convenience I had long dreamed of having—bookshelves from floor to ceiling. Patio doors off the dining area were another dream come true. And a full-sized basement promised our grandchildren a place to romp to their hearts' content.

But could we handle the challenge?

After we had prayed, we made an offer. A compromise was eventually reached, and the house became ours on Washington's birth date. God had worked still another miracle, allowing us to obtain this basically sound dwelling for a third less than it would have cost us to have it built—even by Mr. Carson.

While the Lord has promised to supply all our needs, He didn't promise to deliver them on polished platters. Our needs may be served us on some pretty greasy, grimy serving trays. This was one.

Nonetheless, we were as happy as larks with our investment and began making drives to scrub, scour, paint, paper, and repair. Eventually the interior of the house began to look attractive. Besides, the manual labor was a boon to Buddy's health; the creative endeavor, a release for pent-up tensions.

*　　*　　*

On the morning of the pastoral vote my husband clearly instructed the people to honestly voice their convictions after, of course, having prayed earnestly for divine direction. When the voting was completed and ballots collected, the congregation, pastor, and I waited in suspended silence for the verdict.

Before publicly giving the result, the reporter first showed it to the pastor. Greedily I scanned Buddy's face for an indication. There was none. He remained absolutely expressionless.

Actually it took a moment for me to comprehend the significance of the report after it was given. Nearly twice as many negatives as positives? Incredible!

We were stunned. BUT we had prayed. And we had meant our prayer!

After a period of silence, my husband rose, still remaining expressionless. I wanted to throw my arms around him, to comfort him and assure him of my love and support. But he had to face the crowd and accept the verdict as the will of God—alone. I could only send prayerful, sympathetic, and loving wavelengths to him from the pew.

"Well, now," he said, unruffled, and without a hint of rancor or bitterness, "this is a miracle. It is the first time in all our ministry that this has happend. Thank you for your honesty. I want to assure you we still love you."

145

After I, too, had assured the people of our continued love and Buddy had said, "You are dismissed," I headed for the vestibule as I did after each service. (This time Buddy took the middle aisle.) Why avoid the people? After all, wasn't this the answer we had asked for?

"I still think you're the best pastor's wife in these parts," a loyal member whispered as I turned to leave.

And I needed that!

In the foyer several embraced me. Some cried. Others stared curiously. Yet the Lord was there, enabling me to keep smiling—until I was alone in the parsonage kitchen.

When Buddy came in, the comfort of each other's arms and our mutual reassurances of love for each other erased the tears and eased the hurt. Before I knew it, I was laughing again. In fact, I laughed the rest of that day, for when I thought about it, that vote was so bad, it was ridiculous. So ridiculous it was funny. Still, it was an answer to prayer. Does God have a sense of humor, too?

Telephone calls to our girls and parents brought more consolation and support. When my only sister called late that night and I was still laughing, she said, "I called to cheer you up, but I guess you are making it all right."

However, it was a different story the next morning. Satan had raised his head by then. True, we meant our promises to God and the people. And we intended to keep them. After all, my husband had urged the members to seek the mind of the Lord and vote their convictions. Yet we are human beings and Satan knows it. He wasted no time coming up with suggestions.

"But you've been so kind to everyone!" he prompted.

"We prayed, though. Remember?"

"After all you've sacrificed and they have the gall to do this to you!"

"But we prayed. We can't blame anyone."

Yes, we had borrowed money on our car to buy the household appliances the church was expected to furnish. When salary increases were repeatedly overlooked or rejected, we took it on the chin, without a word of complaint, although many laymen received regular pay raises to offset the rising cost of living.

And what about the devastating trials we had endured because of the housing setup? Often our remarks about the water situation had met with smiles of unconcern. (A few months before we moved, however, action was taken which hopefully and successfully solved the problem for future inhabitants.)

Still, we had prayed!

And what about self-blame? Yes, Satan injected that, too. Where did we go wrong? Where did I fail as a pastor's wife? What did my husband do to deserve this? What is it they hold against him?

"Get thee behind me, Satan!"

And Satan also suggested that we turn on the people, but God enabled us to overcome the temptation to harbor resentment. Divine grace enabled us to rise above the hurt and humiliation.

My husband never changed his attitude toward these people. He continued to preach with a heart of love and understanding. Like Joseph, "he comforted them, and spake kindly unto them" (Gen. 50:21).

Not long after, we received a call to pastor Maple Valley, so he resigned.

Certainly neither of us is a paragon of faultlessness. Our mistakes and shortcomings are many and varied. We make no pretenses whatsoever of being perfect. The people who voted honestly deserve and have our respect. If they sought divine direction as my husband urged (and we have to believe that some did), we can find no fault with them. And as far as the irresponsible ones are concerned, we can only say, again with Joseph, "As for you, ye [may have] thought evil against [us]; but God meant it unto good" (Gen. 50:20).

A short time later we could echo the words of Paul when he declared, "The things which happened unto [us in this assignment] have fallen out rather unto the furtherance of the gospel" (Phil. 1:12). This, too, was a miracle.

*   *   *

The fatal decision concerning Assignment 8 came early in April while we were in the process of renovating our house. Now, knowing we must vacate the parsonage in three months' time, we began pursuing the idea of moving into it instead of renting it out as we had planned. At least we would have a place to live until, and if, another church opened up. Surely the Lord would provide a livelihood of some kind.

One brisk spring day when we went to work on the house, I dropped in to see Ginny. "Did you know Maple Valley's parsonage burned last night?" she asked.

"No!" I answered, shocked.

"I heard it on the news this morning."

"Why don't those people give it up?" I returned, without reflecting. Or was it another premonition I was fighting? Immediately feeling guilty, I asked, "What will they do now?"

Maple Valley, a small country church, located a few miles from the city in which our house was located, had struggled without much notice for years. Since their last pastor had resigned several months before, the congregation was shriveling like a leaf on a frostbitten vine.

But how fortunate now that the parsonage was empty!

"Maybe you'll go there," my friend began hesitatingly. "You could live in your own house . . ."

We? Go there? How could she even suggest it?

We did have to move. That was conclusive. And there was the matter of Buddy's health to consider. Was he able to take on another larger, tension-packed pastorate? Could he endure continued stress? Or was it time for him to accept something with less responsibility?

The idea of moving into our own house strongly appealed to us both. Taking a small church suited Buddy fine. But I wasn't quite ready . . . I still loved a challenge.

Yet the more my husband considered the possibility of pastoring Maple Valley, the more it appealed to him. He increasingly grew more enthusiastic, but I held out. I confess it wasn't easy for me to accept the fact that Buddy's health would not permit him to continue reaching for greener fields. Why did he have to professionally regress at this early stage in life?

But the Holy Spirit kept pushing me into a corner, making me recognize that real success is measured far differently by Him than it is by humanity. There is absolutely no promotion above being in God's will, regardless of the size or prestige of the assignment.

After an intense struggle, I unreservedly yielded my ego ideal to the Lord. I accepted the fact that being where He wanted us was what really counted. Besides, we would be able to live in a house of our own at long last. There are dividends!

We accepted Assignment 9 thinking we were taking a drastic cut in salary, a third less than we had been receiving, but in a very short time this small congregation was practically matching our previous earnings. In addition, they gave us a cost of living increase later on.

Not long after we were ensconced in our new assignment, I ran across a quotation that reinforced my faith. The writer was referring to the apostle Paul when he was forbidden to enter Asia: "The reason for this change in plans was unknown to Paul, but he followed this inner direction or feeling without question. To have followed his own inclination could have limited his ministry. Perhaps his letters to the

Romans and the Corinthians would never have been written. Sometimes the opening of smaller doors than we would have chosen, results in an opportunity to serve God in a much larger way than we had dreamed."

The Lord reminded me that I had prayed for more time to write. He had granted my wish. And there was Buddy's writing to be considered, too.

In addition to that, the people at Maple Valley were a tonic for our broken spirits. We had been through the fire and flood (literally), but a loving Heavenly Father had prepared a quiet resting place for us beside the still waters. We truly felt at home, warmly accepted, loved, and needed.

Miraculously, the picture was completed. And it was not an inert still life but an inviting landscape, filled with beauty and promise. I cannot say our stay was absolutely tension free, but our final assignment was truly enjoyable and, we trust, profitable for the church.

When "Re-fire-ment Day" came, these dear people went all out to make it a gala occasion. Our exodus from the pastoral ministry was a beautiful experience, and it enabled us to begin the next phase of our ministry with happy memories and a sense of fulfillment.

19

Kaleidoscope

People have made me happy, sad, angry, perplexed, brokenhearted, grateful, frustrated, and strangely warmed. If it weren't for people, this confession would never have been made.

Like a twirling kaleidoscope, fragments of the past—serious, stirring, sad, humorous, irritating, baffling, joyous, poignant—slip and slide across my reverie, forming variegated, ever-changing patterns of thought.

* * *

At first I thought I could never do it. Be pastor's wife to Harry and Eva? No way! From my youth I had regarded this talented, sharp-dressing couple with awe.

When we nervously visited their home and were served coffee in fragile china cups, Eva set me at ease by saying, "Don't worry, that's what they are for. Why have pretty things if you can't use them?"

* * *

Esther and James, a young farmer, were married in a simple church wedding. After the ceremony was over, they climbed into a new pickup truck—the bride still wearing her wedding gown and veil and carrying her bouquet.

* * *

Little Mark was an afternoon guest at the parsonage. Back home he said excitedly, "Daddy! Guess what?"

"What?"

"We had green ice cream at Rev. Sprig's house!"

*   *   *

We gratefully accepted the doughnuts Pete brought us from the bakery where he worked nights as a janitor. Our limited income did not allow for bakery items, so we devoured these delicacies with mouth-watering eagerness— until we began biting on grit.

*   *   *

Patty was attracted to the pin I was wearing when we called in her home.

"I got it for Christmas from a relative in Texas," I explained.

"Do they shoot?" she asked pointedly.

*   *   *

What fun we had pulling old-fashioned taffy when I entertained my teenage Sunday School class in the parsonage! The grease stain on the dining room wallpaper served as a reminder for many months to come, however.

*   *   *

Who could forget the little lady with the big voice? She sang so loudly and off-key that she threw the entire congregation into a dither. The song director could neither outsing nor out-direct her. And the people could not drown her out— or stay on key when she pulled out the stops. We were in a quandary. Besides, we couldn't keep the youngsters (and some of the oldsters) from laughing.

When Dot bewailed to me about the smiles, I suggested as tactfully as possible that she try singing very softly. But she insisted she couldn't refrain from singing when she came to church. Nor could she control her voice.

Peace came, sadly enough, when she stopped attending.

* * *

Asked to dismiss a prayer service, Peggy besought the Lord to "bless those we love and those who are good for us."

* * *

Treena, a brand-new Christian, was exhorting the young folk. "If you think this is a pretty bad world," she said in all seriousness, "by golly, it's worse if you're not a Christian!"

* * *

Christmas programs! How well they managed to turn out despite the chaos on Saturday afternoon! One year the young adult play was destined to flop until the very last minute. Then the leading character made cue cards and placed them inconspicuously on the floor. Another propped his book up in the manger. Everyone was astonished at the successful performance. Only a few knew our secret.

* * *

When invited to a tea at an "elite" church in town, I asked a friend to accompany me. We dressed to the hilt, hoping to put in a satisfactory appearance. Barbara picked me up on a wintry February afternoon. We drove across town in her car and parked beside a snowbank.

"Looks like we're the first ones here," she said.

So we sat in the car and waited. And waited. And waited.

Finally when no one else arrived, we began to question it. Then it dawned on us. We had chosen the wrong day. In fact, we were a week early. Naturally, I succumbed to laughter, but my friend begged, "Don't tell anyone about this!" (It's OK, ———, I used a pseudonym.)

*   *   *

During another assignment, we were privileged to see two brothers converted and join the church. Quickly they were given small, "important" jobs to do. Soon after, both of them came to church carrying brand-new briefcases.

*   *   *

A teenaged Mexican boy got saved and never missed a service, often coming early to help tidy up the sanctuary. "I don't like church," he declared; "I love it!"

Late one evening this fatherless lad came to the parsonage. "I want to see Rev. Spray," he said, explaining that his mother had sent him to talk to the pastor.

"I have a question to ask you," he told my husband. "It's very silly." He grinned, his white teeth flashing in his handsome, dark face. "Ees eet all right for me to have a girlfriend? To write notes to and sit with?"

"Is she a nice girl?"

"Oh, she ees very nice!"

I smiled behind the newspaper I was reading.

*   *   *

Jennie took up hair dressing in later life. One Sunday morning she arrived at church with snarls to spare. In her haste she had forgotten to comb her own hair. How she must have felt when she made the discovery!

*   *   *

Bella furnished Kleenex for the runny-nosed kids attending Sunday School. She also kept the older people in line with her sharp tongue. When it was twelve o'clock—visiting ministers or whom-have-you notwithstanding—she arose from her pew near the front and with exaggerated motion put her coat on over the sweater she wore each Sunday for months on end. If the service wasn't dismissed by the time she had made her elaborate preparations, she stalked down the aisle and headed for home.

*   *   *

Polly lived on the run. She ran to the parsonage with meat after they butchered. She ran over with a pie or loaf of bread. And she ran to church, waving at the people as she ran down the aisle. Before sitting down, she adjusted the venetian blind so she could see her porch light. If her husband needed her, he would turn it on. Periodically she got up during the service to check.

Once a former pastor's wife asked, "Does the lady with the wart on her tongue still go there?"

Until then I had not noticed the wart, but Polly was such a dear I would have loved her if she had had warts all over.

*   *   *

Without a doubt I pulled my worst boner during an early assignment when it was necessary for me to act as Sunday School superintendent.

"We're glad to have Jim and Dora here this morning with their new baby," I exclaimed brightly. "How about showing us your new addition?"

Obligingly, Jim stood up with a broad, proud grin and unveiled the newcomer. The audience ohed and ahed and craned their necks for a glimpse of the little one.

"Having a baby is one way of increasing our attendance," I said with a smile. And then in closing, I added thoughtlessly, "Now everyone go home and get busy this week."

Pandemonium broke loose.

*   *   *

How we laughed when Lucy, an important bank employee, showed up at a wedding reception with the cleaner's tag still attached to her dress!

* * *

What fun we had watching "Mama" and "I Love Lucy" when television was young and more wholesome. Before we owned a set, we joined the Potters in their living room and shared laughs and buttered popcorn.

* * *

Thurman was faithful to pray for his pastor. "Lord, bless him as he 'repares his sermon," he petitioned many times.

* * *

I never hear the hymn "Anywhere with Jesus," but I am reminded of one lady who often requested it. The last verse was truly apropos, for she fell asleep during every service: "Anywhere with Jesus I can go to sleep . . ."

Her weakness was quite naturally a source of amusement to others. Wes approached this dear soul after one of her "peaceful" evenings and asked, "Mrs. Anson, how did you enjoy the service tonight?" knowing full well she had been in slumberland most of the time.

* * *

While visiting a patient in a hospital ward, my husband read some scripture and offered prayer. We started to leave the room when a feeble old lady at the far end raised up in bed and said in broken English, "I tink you for you prayer."

* * *

Helen sat in the same pew Sunday after Sunday—next to the outside aisle on the south side of the church. After she died suddenly, someone asked her daughter, "Mary, how do you stand it to go to church when your mother isn't there?"

"That's easy," she replied. "I go and sit in her pew."

* * *

Godfrey had difficulty keeping the front of his trousers zipped. Usually his fly was about at half-mast. However, he was a good man and dearly loved to work for the Lord. On visitation nights he was one of our most enthusiastic and faithful workers. Nevertheless, we hesitated to send him out calling on strangers because of his carelessness in dress.

Each week we met at the church to pray before going out to visit. One evening I noticed Godfrey's embarrassing condition and called my husband aside to tell him.

Buddy moved up to the offender, slipped a friendly arm around the man's shoulders, and with the other hand surreptitiously retrieved the slipped fastener.

I doubt if Godfrey was the wiser.

*   *   *

No youngster was ever prouder of an instrument than Johnny was of his baritone. Although the horn looked like someone had taken a can opener to it, the bright-eyed youngster seemed oblivious to its condition when he stopped by the parsonage to leave it in our care.

*   *   *

Mrs. Jacobs resided in an old, dilapidated hotel which had been made into a retirement center for the poor and elderly. To reach her room a rickety, ancient elevator jerked us to an upper floor. There we found her ensconced in her limited world—bed, dresser, bathroom, and a few personal belongings. "I'm just hoping I'll die in my sleep some night," she sighed plaintively. But her otherwise peppery language, her ample-sized body, and the fire in her eyes said quite the contrary.

Her obviously assumed tone of voice, plus the fact that she also talked about taking medication and seeing the doctor, struck me as being humorous. Later that evening I laughingly told the Cobbs about our visit when we called on them.

157

"Do you know who you're talking about?" he asked. "She's my sister."

Well . . . I still thought it was funny!

*   *   *

After taking a small gift to tiny, black-eyed Lisa in the hospital, we received the following note: THANK YOU FOR THE PENCILS AND PAPER AND GUM I AM GETTING A LOT BETTER LOVE LISA. I still cherish that printed message made with a blue pencil on purple paper.

*   *   *

On a frigid February Sunday, following the morning service, Harry passed us and honked as we turned into our snowbanked drive. It was the first time he had ever done that. On Tuesday, a couple of days later, his wife returned home from work to find him dead in bed.

*   *   *

After many years Doris still fondly remembers the Halloween night when she and I dressed up and went trick-or-treating, calling on several of the elderly church people, who laughingly welcomed us masquerading adults.

*   *   *

I've never fogotten the impromptu meal we enjoyed with the Tawney family years ago. Having dropped in uninvited early one Saturday afternoon, we found this happy troupe about to eat a late lunch of pancakes—and dill pickles. They insisted we join them at their bare-topped table. My, how we enjoyed both the food and the congenial fellowship.

*   *   *

Our first introduction to pizza came when a newly wedded couple invited us to their home. They served it with—of all things—hot tea. After 20 years of being out of touch, Don and Margaret called us one Saturday night not so long ago. They had lost track of us but successfully ran us down through the assistance of telephone operators. Shortly thereafter, we were saddened to learn of Don's passing.

*   *   *

Personally, I found it rewarding to call with my husband (although I detested making visits to the mental hospital where we were locked in). I enjoyed visiting in the homes of our people and getting to know them better. Nowadays clerical spouses—the majority, no doubt—seldom accompany their husbands on his rounds. Many do not consider it the professional thing to do. Others work or are homebound with young children. But I think they miss a lot. Few are as eagerly welcomed as the pastor and his wife. Being received with open arms is one of the compensations afforded "the called of God."

I must confess, however, that sometimes I trudged along unwillingly. I have gone calling on the sick when I was so weary I gladly would have crawled into one of the empty hospital beds. Nevertheless, accompanying my husband gave me many interesting memories.

*   *   *

One church had begun as a mission. Some of the people who attended still lived in sad circumstances. Nonetheless, it was remarkable how a woman could come to church looking like she had just stepped out of a band box—immaculately dressed, including hat and white gloves—and still reside as she did in a hovel scarcely fit for human habitation.

One of those houses I shall never forget. Sitting in a smelly, muddy yard, it was surrounded by an open trench, an alluring invitation to unwanted rodents. Inside, a battered conglomeration of furniture, piles of disheveled clothing, dirty dishes, grimy stoves, and loaded tables crowded out the untidy shack.

But the outstanding feature, a vision I shall always carry, was an empty tomato can (with paper intact) which was secured to the kitchen ceiling by an ample-sized nail driven through the partially attached lid. The purpose for which the can was spiked there I have never been able to figure out. Perhaps the roof leaked, but if so, what did they do when the can filled with water?

*   *   *

Another lady was faithful in bringing several of her 11 children to Sunday School. Her husband never showed up—at church, that is. He spent most of his time in the penitentiary, excepting for brief intervals, as the size of his family indicated.

*   *   *

Vi, too, was forced to live in poor conditions, although she was a lovely person and made an honest effort to live as decently as possible. For quite some time she was forced to reside in a dilapidated building that had previously served as a church for a black congregation. The huge rooms were not only unattractive but drafty and frigid in the wintertime. Once when we called, we found the family huddled around the open oven of the battered kitchen range, trying to escape the freezing wind that blew through the cracks and crevices.

When one of Vi's teenage daughters got involved with a married man, this poor woman was saddled with another burden. Although the baby died at birth, still Vi grieved. After all, the newborn child was her flesh and blood, too.

My husband conducted the graveside service while the young mother, just out of the hospital, and the father stood in the snow holding hands.

The Lord poured a special measure of love for Vi into my heart. Warmed by His Spirit, I felt especially drawn to this unfortunate soul; and when we called to comfort her, it was easy to embrace her and place a kiss on her careworn cheek.

*   *   *

Grandma Wilson lived not far away in the same area. Calling on this dear old lady was pure pleasure, for her conversations from start to finish were sprinkled liberally with praise. Even on her deathbed she feebly raised a wrinkled hand and whispered, "Praise the Lord." Although she lived in a mighty poor dwelling here on earth, I'm sure she's inhabiting a colossal mansion in heaven—and still shouting God's praises.

*   *   *

One of my favorite recollections dates back to a time when I was ill and unable to attend the morning worship service. Just before leaving the house, Buddy looked at me wistfully and said, "I've been working on a new sermon, and I hate to waste it if you're not there."

*   *   *

And so "we [have spent] our years as a tale that is told" (Ps. 90:9)—and the kaleidoscope keeps twirling on. It would be impossible to tell of all that has happened to us in the ministry. So long as we live, scenes from our past will flash across the screen of memory. As the Psalmist said, "The lines [have] fallen unto me in pleasant places" (16:6). The somber tones have only served to accentuate the brightly colored spaces.

20

Paper, Pencil—and Perseverance

Writing isn't a breeze by any means. Nor is it all glamour and acclaim. It involves perseverance and perspiration as well as inspiration and incandescent ideas.

A chronicle of our life together would be incomplete without making mention of the miracles God has performed where our writing is concerned.

My first published work appeared as a letter to the "Children's Page" of the *God's Revivalist* before I was 7. At 12 I made another literary attempt when I wrote the following poem for my mother:

> *Who is the sweetest one on earth?*
> *My mother.*
> *Who loved and cared for me from birth?*
> *My mother.*
> *Who kept me from the cold and blast?*
> *My mother.*
> *My love for her will ever last.*
> *My mother.*

During my high school years someone asked, "Pauline, what do you plan to do when you're out of school?"

"I'm going to be a writer," I answered brashly.

But a couple of teachers must have recognized a smidgen of promise, for they encouraged and abetted me in my youthful attempts.

Then several years passed. Thought of becoming a writer was eclipsed by romance, marriage, and the birth of our first child.

While Sybil was still a baby, inspiration struck again, however, but that bit of composition reposes unfinished in my desk drawer. I keep it for sentimental purposes.

Following that, Sue was born. And Buddy was called to preach. When he entered the ministry, any desire to write was sublimated by the thrill of becoming a minister's wife.

When I was in my early 30s, my health broke. While passing through this personal Gethsemane, I discovered that being a pastor's wife, although a full-time job in itself, was not enough. To realize personal fulfillment I needed an additional outlet for my creative energies, an individualized means of venting my tensions. Unless released constructively, they backed up, causing mental and emotional problems.

About this time a friend recommended Glenn Clark's book, *I Will Lift Up Mine Eyes,* and I ordered it. As soon as it arrived, I began reading eagerly. But I must confess my prejudices prevented my wholehearted acceptance of its message. Nevertheless, the Lord was prepared to remove my questions.

Having perused the introductory chapter and the first day's devotional message, I turned to the scripture reference for the day. Opening to Proverbs 8 as directed, I read the first 32 verses. Nothing happened.

But the 33rd verse smote me with a persuasive force. My hesitancy vanished like smoke in the wind.

"Hear instruction, and be wise, and refuse it not!" Solomon's words penetrated my darkness with fluorescent rays.

"Hear instruction, and be wise, and refuse it not!" With this divine injunction ringing in my ears I returned greedily to Mr. Clark's book.

Then I glanced again at the scripture reference for the day. "Psalm 8! Not Proverbs 8?" Were my eyes deceiving me? How could I have erred?

The Lord had used a mistake (or was it?) to work a miracle, directing me to the exact message I needed.

This author, I discovered, believed that dreams do come true. He pointed out that the first step toward turning fancy into reality involves finding out just what your "soul's sincere desire" really is. It helps, he maintained, to look into one's childhood. What did one dream of becoming then? Childhood dreams come the closest to being God-implanted desires, so he believed.

After identifying one's "soul's sincere desire," one must surrender it completely to God. If it agrees with His will, He will return it in His own way and time.

So I did just that. "O Lord," I prayed, "I am giving my dream of writing to You. If it is Your will, bring it to pass in Your own time and way." After praying sincerely, I put the thought out of my mind.

Several months later we moved.

In *Daily Delights* I told of the incident that started it all. At the Bush and Lane upright Sybil chopped out the strains of a well-known hymn. Standing beside her, Sue sang lustily, "All hail the power of Jesus' name! Let angels prostrate fall. Bring forth the royal dynamite . . ."

"Royal dynamite?" We laughed.

Despite my amusement, I thought: There's an article in that! Faith is "royal dynamite." It moves mountains. So I sat down at the dining room table and began writing. The words flowed easily. God, then and there, gave back to me what I had relinquished to Him months before.

My husband praised my article and insisted I submit it to the local paper. In fact, he took it in himself. The editor liked it, too, and published it immediately. And, at Buddy's insistence, I sent it to our church paper. That editor also used it.

Following "instant" success—another miracle—I promised the Lord I would jot down the ideas that came to me. And they began coming thick and fast.

When I told the editor of our denominational magazine about my frequent inspirations, he replied graciously, "Whenever you have an inspiration, write it out and send it to me."

From then on my articles and stories have appeared in that publication and other papers many times, thanks to a magnanimous man who took the time and made the effort to encourage a blushing novice.

Nevertheless, that was only the beginning. There was so much to learn. I knew that if I were to first master all the great literary works, knowhow, and techniques of writing, I would be years getting started. So I chose to begin just where I was. Writing. Rewriting. Submitting manuscripts. And getting them back. Redoing many. Sending them out again. And again. Learning by trial and error. Swallowing my pride. Overcoming humiliation and discouragement. Developing the hide of a rhinoceros and the perseverance of a worker ant.

Gradually I became acquainted with a few published authors who egged me on and offered valuable suggestions.

"When your children are gone," an older woman assured me, "you'll still have your brainchild." I often think of her sage observation when threatened by lonesomeness.

Again, a quotation from Glenn Clark was invaluable. He said that each of us has access to the same sources of originality that great writers, including Shakespeare, had. These, he said, are our reminiscences, prejudices, and convictions. We must be true to our own personality. Dip into these reservoirs honestly and sincerely. Point our words. Put rhythm into our sentences. If we do these things, we are bound to come up with something worthwhile.

I confess that being true to one's own personality calls for courage. It is a genuine challenge to let one's real self shine through, to expose one's innermost being to public scrutiny, revealing, if necessary, one's faults, weaknesses, neuroticisms, humanness, peculiarities, and so on. This, I also confess, is not the easiest thing to do.

After I had been writing a few years, I began to feel burdened to write for the newspaper. Many people, I believed, who wouldn't be caught dead reading a Bible or Christian publication, might stealthfully peruse a spiritual truth behind a yawning daily. So I began to pray about it.

A brief time later we moved again. Shortly thereafter, I contacted the editor of the local paper. He immediately requested an interview. With fear, trembling, and fervent prayer, I met him and got the job I wanted. Writing an inspirational column for a wide circulation for 3½ years was one of the most rewarding experiences of my life.

"I've never done anything like this before," the scholarly gentleman explained over the phone. "I've never made a call or written a fan letter before, but I wanted you to know how much I enjoy your column. Please don't stop writing."

That substantiated what I had believed in the beginning.

Within a few years 366 of those "Homespun Devotions" came out in book form, entitled *Daily Delights*. The same year *Planned Programs for Women's Groups* also appeared in print.

While looking for another writing project, I recalled a conversation I had had with a friend. After telling her about my breakdown and how God had brought healing to me through His Word, she said emphatically, "Pauline, you've got to write about that!"

Since her suggestion kept ringing in my ears, I decided to give it a try. Nevertheless, I must confess that a similitude of a start graphically revealed there was a lot I did not know about my subject. Were my theories psychologically and scientifically, as well as biblically, sound? Much research was needed, I soon discovered.

But almost at once the Lord began working miracles. He sent people to offer inspiration and illustrative material. Some loaned me invaluable books on the subject. *Rx for "Nerves"* began unfolding.

After five years of research, writing, and rewriting, I came up with a voluminous manuscript. Although the editor had expressed interest in seeing it, he returned the copy promptly because of its size.

The disappointing bundle was waiting for us when we returned from vacation in the middle of June. Besides helping in Vacation Bible School and attending a week of church activities, the Lord miraculously enabled me to cut the manuscript to one-third its original size, retype, and return it to the editor by the middle of August.

"You have accomplished the well-nigh impossible by reducing the size of your manuscript as you have done," he wrote.

Out of the remnant of the original manuscript was salvaged two more books: *How to Live with Less Tension* and *Rx for Happiness*. Participation in a senior adult retreat resulted in *The Autumn Years*.

Nearly 25 years after my first article was published in our church paper, another one appeared in a special issue, accompanied by an editorial note, which began, "Pauline Spray, well known to [our] readers . . ."

To whom, really, was the editor referring? Certainly not that naive dreamer who had dashed off her first article to his publication after hearing her little girl sing about "royal dynamite"! Not the shy, self-conscious, inferiority-stricken lass who declared brashly, "I'm going to be a writer"!

But that's where the miracle of it all comes in. God has always delighted in using ordinary people to work for Him. Furthermore, He can take the least promising person and work miracles through him (or her) if that person is totally yielded to His melting and molding—and is willing to persistently work at his task.

One of my greatest compensations came when a missionary to Africa told me that she had been teaching my book, *Rx for "Nerves,"* to the national women.

Dreams can come true.

Dreams do come true!

Recently I received a note from Blanche Eastman, the lady who introduced me to Glenn Clark early in our ministry. She wrote, "For years I have thought of expressing my joy that your dream has come true. It was at a zone rally . . . in the basement of the church [where] you told me of your heart's desire. To see it unfold has been a delight."

But that isn't the end of the story. Following my husband's illness during Assignment 8, the Lord opened up an additional avenue of service for him, also. Ever since beginning to preach, he had avidly studied sermon outline books. They fascinated him. And he often expressed the desire to compile his originals.

Until experiencing his own Gethsemane, this urge had remained a misty dream. Now he was driven to do something about making it a reality. Subsequently, by dint of determination, diligent effort, and divine assistance, he has achieved his goal. In fact, his fondest hopes have been surpassed. His 14th book recently came off the press . . . and there are more to come.

Some time ago permission was granted for his outline books to be translated into the Indonesian language and distributed to needy pastors and laymen in that faraway area. Promises are they will be a special blessing to those "in the hinterland."

And that's still another miracle!

—21—

Final Touch

"I never dreamed when I was getting married, a little boy was being born who would grow up to marry my first daughter," Ma said, after she found out about it herself years later. True, the very day my parents exchanged their "I wills" in Grandma's goldenrod-bedecked parlor, Buddy came to enliven the home of his parents in southeastern Oklahoma.

When he was 16, he began singing and playing his mandolin for the Lord. Eventually, his travels brought him to the North—and me.

Despite the distance that divided us, God worked a miracle and led us to each other. Certainly ours was not the customary type of courtship. But the Heavenly Father is not restricted to the conventional. He uses many ways and means to promote the cause of Jesus Christ here on earth.

"All things work together for good," the apostle Paul declared, "to them that love God, to them who are the called . . ." (Rom. 8:28).

Now as I look back over my life—over 45 years of marriage, over 32 as a pastor's wife—I confess that there have been many things I did not understand at the time. But the longer I live, the clearer the picture becomes with the viewing.

Two things are certain: I have always loved the Lord. He became my personal Savior when I was a young child. Second, I am among "the called." For also as a child, while sitting on the arm of Ma's oaken rocker, God laid His hand on my life and called me to special service. That indelible impression, an unshakable conviction, has never left me. A sense of responsibility, a weight of oughtness, continues to rest on my shoulders to this present time. And I expect that only death will terminate it.

We had been married for several years and had two children when my husband was called to preach. God's appointment for him caused my own cup to overflow with happiness, too. Since the day he took his first pastorate, we have been privileged to know some of the best people on earth. Our hearts have been warmed by the love of Mabels, Myrtles, Marthas, Harolds, Ellies, Ivas, Emerys, Thelmas, Russells, Shirleys, Lindas, Jeffs, Helens, Kens, Bettys, Rons, Verlas, Esthers, Clydes, Ories, Freds, Cleos, Nylas, Charlottes, Dales, Jerrys, Ellens, Bobs, Audreys, Berthas, Williams, Elsies—and the list runs on—endlessly.

While a few people have caused the tears to flow, many others have flooded our lives with sunshine and kindnesses. We have enjoyed the fellowship of some of God's finest laity. Certainly we have not always rejoiced with exceeding great joy over the trials that came. Nor have we liked everything about every assignment. Nevertheless, the compensations have far exceeded any price we have had to pay.

One dignitary told about a preacher's wife who died. The notice in the bulletin was supposed to say, "She's gone to claim the promises." It read instead: "She's gone to clean the premises."

My appreciation goes to all those dear souls who labored so industriously to give us clean houses into which to move. And double appreciation goes to those who scrubbed up after we departed.

Truly I am deeply touched when I recall the sacrifices people (in every assignment) have made for us—the meals brought in on moving day; the restaurant entertaining; gifts to us and our girls; hospital remembrances; birthday, anniversary, welcome, and farewell parties which were given in our honor.

I have been as eager as the children to see "what they brought us" when a member dropped by with a sack of groceries or a freshly baked goody.

The produce from the gardens of the Archies, Beechers, Evelyns, Marcias, and Roberts have helped fill the jars on our shelves year after year. And the generosity of our good friends keeps flowing in.

Each autumn when I can vegetables, I still use the canner Beulah gave "her pastor" and me. And each Christmas I use Bertha's recipe when I make decorated sugar cookies for our grandchildren. No holiday season is complete without them.

And when we have to make up extra beds for our children and grandchildren, we use the comforters and quilts made for us by the kindly women of that first assignment when we were still rookies.

I remember, too, being awakened by the sound of Plynn's shovel or snowblower on Sunday morning as he cleared paths for the people who would come to worship.

One morning Bea woke up feeling depressed. She decided to make a visit to the parsonage, hoping it would lift her troubled spirits. On the way she stopped at the florist shop and purchased a pretty planter.

I had been ill and welcomed her in my housecoat.

"Here's a little something to cheer you up," she said, handing me the arrangement.

"Do you know what day this is?" I asked.

"No, what?"

"It's our anniversary. Come on in."

We prayed and read the Bible, and she went away feeling uplifted. Years later she said that was one day she would never forget. We were special people in her life. And needless to say, she was a special blessing to us that day, too.

Another time the doorbell rang. When I answered it, there stood Becky with a beautiful, blue glass bowl, an anniversary gift from the congregation.

Maxine's husband had just undergone back surgery so he was barred from heavy lifting. Still, she wanted me to have a set of ancient encyclopedias I had coveted. I cringe at the thought of her toting that heavy load when she herself was in need of surgery, but her expression of love is warmly remembered and cherished.

And there was the day when Les knocked on our kitchen door. When I opened it, he held out a gorgeous antique dish.

"I saw this at a sale and thought of you," he said.

When it came time to move into our own home, Les and his son used their trailer, working long and hard to spare us the expense of a van. Later on, he and his brother put new siding on our retirement home.

At Christmastime when we have stood before the people to receive the gift from the congregation, I have felt especially humble and unworthy. Always I have been made aware of my failures throughout the year. As gratitude has welled up in my heart, I have wanted to throw my arms around "our brood" and tell them how much we loved and appreciated each one.

Nor do they forget when we move on. We still receive occasional long-distance phone calls, and the birthday and anniversary cards continue to come year after year.

And since the procuring of our own little home, a group of missionary-minded men from a former assignment drove many miles to put a new roof on our house. After working several hours in the chilly rain, they gave my husband a check for $100 to help defray the expense of the shingles.

172

*　　*　　*

No doubt each profession has its own reward. As for the preacher's wife, hers is unique. Nothing can replace the awesome pleasure she receives when a little girl fixes an adoring gaze on her. Diamonds? Pearls? Robes of ermine? None compares with that compensation! Or the thrill she receives when she leads a soul to Christ! Or when she inspires others to reach for God's highest and best!

All too often we are unaware of our influence. When we left Assignment 4, one of the Sunday School children gave us a card she had made and decorated brightly. In pencil she had written: "Dear Mr. and Mrs. Spray, I will miss you very much. I like both of you very much, too. From Birdie."

We scarcely knew Birdie. But Birdie knew us.

Three weeks before Betty, the wife of one of the men whom Buddy encouraged to prepare for the ministry, died, Jean called on her in the hospital. During their conversation, she said, "There's only one person in the world I would want to be like. That's Pauline."

Could anyone ask for greater remuneration?

*　　*　　*

Yes, I confess that life has been very good to me. I'm mighty glad I fell in love at first sight—with God. And with my husband.

The final touch:

Heavenly Father, in the rehearsing of this story, we have endeavored to show "to the generation to come [Your] praises . . . and [Your] strength, and [Your] wonderful works . . . that they might set their hope in [You] . . . [and] keep [Your] commandments" (Ps. 78:4, 7).

May the name of our Lord Jesus Christ be glorified! This is my prayer!